Colin Wilson's
'Occult Trilogy'

A Guide for Students

Colin Wilson's 'Occult Trilogy'

A Guide for Students

Colin Stanley

AXIS MUNDI
BOOKS

Winchester, UK
Washington, USA

First published by Axis Mundi Books, 2013
Axis Mundi Books is an imprint of John Hunt Publishing Ltd., Laurel House, Station Approach,
Alresford, Hants, SO24 9JH, UK
office1@jhpbooks.net
www.johnhuntpublishing.com
www.axismundi-books.com

For distributor details and how to order please visit the 'Ordering' section on our website.

Text copyright: Colin Stanley 2012

ISBN: 978 1 84694 706 3

A CIP catalogue record for this book is available from the British Library.

Design: Stuart Davies

Printed and bound by CPI Group (UK) Ltd, Croydon, CR0 4YY

We operate a distinctive and ethical publishing philosophy in all
areas of our business, from our global network of authors to
production and worldwide distribution.

CONTENTS

Acknowledgements

❀

Colin Wilson for permission to quote from his books.
The author also acknowledges helpful suggestions from
George Poulos on the subject of split brain research
in the chapter on *Beyond the Occult*.

Preface

❀

Colin Wilson's 'Occult Trilogy' is the collective label applied to his three major works on the occult which were published between the years 1971 and 1988:

- *The Occult* (1971)
- *Mysteries: an Investigation into the Occult, the Paranormal and the Supernatural* (1978)
- *Beyond the Occult* (1988)

The three books amount to a monumental 1600 pages and spawned many other lesser works on the subject (all of which are listed in the checklist at the end of this book).

In the opening chapter of *The Occult* Wilson recounts that as a twenty-year-old, living in rented accommodation in London with his wife and young child, working in various dead-end factory jobs, he read all the books on magic and mysticism that he could find in libraries not just as an escape from his lot but "...because they confirmed my intuition of another order of reality, *an intenser and more powerful form of consciousness* than the kind I seemed to share" (46*). By the time he came to write *The Occult*, in the late 1960s, he had accumulated a library of "...five hundred or so volumes on magic and the supernatural" (40) but did not consider the occult to be "...one of my major interests, like philosophy or science, or even music" (40). However, all this preliminary reading obviously stood him in good stead when the book was commissioned and he duly set about researching the subject more systematically. As a result he began to become convinced that "...the basic claims of 'occultism' are true." (41):

"In the past few centuries, science has made us aware that the universe is stranger and more interesting than our ancestors realised. It is an amusing thought that it may turn out stranger and more interesting than even the scientists are willing to admit." (41)

As I pointed out in the Preface to my guide to Colin Wilson's 'Outsider Cycle' (*Colin Wilson's* Outsider Cycle: *a guide for students*. Nottingham: Paupers' Press, 2009) his style of writing renders the books eminently readable (even when dealing with the most challenging of subjects), so much so that attempts at elucidation can often have the opposite effect. For that reason I have tried to quote him as often as practicable with the minimum of comment from myself.

All three books have recently been reprinted by Watkins Publishing, with new Introductions by Wilson.

Colin Stanley
Nottingham, UK
May 2012

*All page references are from the Mayflower Books Ltd paperback edition of *The Occult*. St Albans: Mayflower Books Ltd., 1973 (1976 reprint).

Notes

❁

In **Bibliographical Details**, citations under *Secondary Sources and Reviews* to Around, Bendau, Bergstrom, Campion, Celebration, Dossor, and Weigel, refer to the following critical monographs on Wilson's work:

- **Around**: *Around the Outsider: essays presented to Colin Wilson on the occasion of his 80th birthday* edited by Colin Stanley. Winchester: O-Books, 2011.
- **Bendau**: *Colin Wilson: The Outsider and Beyond* by Clifford P. Bendau. San Bernardino, CA: The Borgo Press, 1979.
- **Bergstrom**: *An Odyssey to Freedom: Four Themes in Colin Wilson's Novels* by K. Gunnar Bergström. [Acta Universitatis Upsaliensis, Studia Anglistica Upsaliensia, no. 47] Uppsala, Sweden: University of Uppsala, 1983.
- **Campion**: *The World of Colin Wilson* by Sidney Campion. London: Frederick Müller, 1962.
- **Celebration**: *Colin Wilson, a Celebration: Essays and Recollections* edited by Colin Stanley. London: Cecil Woolf, 1988.
- **Dossor**: *Colin Wilson: the Man and his Mind* by Howard F. Dossor. Shaftesbury, Dorset: Element Books, 1990.
- **Weigel**: *Colin Wilson* by John A. Weigel [Twayne English Author Series, no. 181]. Boston: Twayne Publishers, 1975.

References are also made to various *Colin Wilson Studies*, edited by Colin Stanley (Nottingham: Paupers' Press):

- Moorhouse/Newman: *C.W. Study #1. Colin Wilson, two essays: 'The English Existentialist' and 'Spiders and Outsiders'* by John Moorhouse and Paul Newman. 1989.

- Stanley: **C.W. Study** *#2*. *'The Nature of Freedom' and other essays* by Colin Stanley. 1990.
- Trowell: **C.W. Study** *#3*. *Colin Wilson, the positive Approach: a response to a critic* by Michael Trowell. 1990.
- Smalldon: **C.W. Study** *#4*. *Human Nature Stained: Colin Wilson and the existential study of modern murder* by Jeffrey Smalldon. 1991.
- Dalgleish: **C.W. Study** *#5*. *The Guerilla Philosopher: Colin Wilson and Existentialism* by Tim Dalgleish. 1993.
- Lachman: **C.W. Study** *#6*. *Two Essays on Colin Wilson: 'World Rejection and Criminal Romantics' and 'From Outsider to Post-Tragic Man'* by Gary Lachman. 1994.
- Shand/Lachman: **C.W. Study** *#8*. *'Colin Wilson as Philosopher' and 'Faculty X, Consciousness and the Transcendence of Time'* by John Shand and Gary Lachman. 1996.
- Dossor: **C.W. Study** *#9*. *The Philosophy of Colin Wilson: three perspectives* by Howard F. Dossor. 1996.
- Robertson: **C.W. Study** *#11*. *Wilson as Mystic* by Vaughan Robertson. 2001.
- Campion (2): **C.W. Study** *#19*. *The Sound Barrier* by Sidney Campion. 2011.

nd = date not known.

nk = page numbers not known.

All bibliographical details extracted from: *The Colin Wilson Bibliography, 1956-2010* by Colin Stanley [Colin Wilson Studies #17]. Nottingham: Paupers' Press, 2011.

Book 1: *The Occult*

❈

The Occult was Colin Wilson's first commissioned book and he made no secret of the fact that, at first, it was not a subject that interested him greatly. When he sought the advice of Robert Graves on whether he should write it, he was told very firmly that he should not. However, with a young family to support, Wilson needed the money and fortunately went ahead with the project. During the course of his research, he found his attitude to the subject changing:

> "Although I have always been curious about the 'occult'...it has never been one of my major interests, like philosophy, or science, or even music.... It was not until two years ago, when I began the systematic research for this book, that I realised the remarkable consistency of the evidence for such matters as life after death, out-of-body experiences (astral projection), reincarnation. In a basic sense my attitude remains unchanged; I still regard philosophy—the pursuit of reality through intuition aided by intellect—as being more *relevant* more important, than questions of the 'occult'. But the weighing of the evidence...has convinced me that the basic claims of 'occultism' are true." (40-41*)

The completed book, dedicated to Graves, was published on October 4, 1971, by Hodder & Stoughton in the U.K. and Random House in the U.S. In his new Introduction to a 2003 reprint, published by Watkins Publishing, he wrote, "The publication of this book had the effect of changing my life". Cyril Connolly and Philip Toynbee who, as critics, were instrumental in turning his *The Outsider* into a bestseller in 1956, but had subsequently changed their minds and then ignored his work for fifteen years, relaxed their embargo and came out in support of him again.

"But for me, *The Occult* did a great deal more than make me 'respectable', it also served as a kind of awakening. Before 1970, I had been inclined to dismiss 'the occult' as superstitious nonsense. Writing *The Occult* made me aware that the paranormal is as real as quantum physics (and, in fact, has a great deal in common with it), and that anyone who refuses to take it into account is simply shutting his eyes to half the universe." (Wilson (1), xxii)

A huge book (over 600 pages), it became the first in a trilogy of equally bulky volumes on the subject. *Mysteries* followed in 1978 (London: Hodder and Stoughton) and *Beyond the Occult* (London, New York: Bantam Press) in 1988. The book also spawned numerous popular, illustrated books on the subject which have been issued under his name since the 1970s and, indeed, continue to appear today [see following checklist].

The Occult is divided into three parts, preceded by a short Introduction. The first part, 'A Survey of the Subject', states Wilson's own preoccupations and convictions. The second, 'A History of Magic', concentrates on individual 'mages' and adepts. The third part, 'Man's Latent Powers', looks at witchcraft, spiritualism and ghosts with a final chapter that discusses the metaphysical questions that arise out of occultism.

"The thesis of this book is revolutionary..." Wilson declares on the first page of his Introduction (25*). Primitive man believed the world to be full of unseen forces whereas today our rational minds tell us that these forces existed only in his imagination. The problem, says Wilson, is that we have become "thinking pigmies" who have forgotten "the immense world of broader significance that stretches around [us]" (25). It is his belief that civilisation cannot evolve until the occult is taken for granted "on the same level as atomic energy" (27) and he recommends that we re-learn the technique of expanding inwardly and relax our hard-headed approach to subjects such as premonition, life after death etc.

"Man has reached a point in his evolution where he must...turn increasingly inward. That is, he must turn to the hidden levels of his being, to the 'occult', to meanings and vibrations that have so far been too fine to grasp." (38)

He claims that the science of cybernetics has suggested that there is a certain order and meaning behind the universe and that:

"All this means that for the first time in Western history a book on the occult can be something more than a collection of marvels and absurdities. Religion, mysticism and magic all spring from the same basic 'feeling' about the universe: a sudden feeling of meaning...." (34)

In Part 1, Chapter 1, which has the seemingly paradoxical title 'Magic—The Science of the Future', Wilson explains that although he had read books on magic and mysticism in his youth, he did so "because they confirmed my intuition of another order of reality, *an intenser and more powerful form of consciousness*..." (46). But if, at that time, he had been asked whether he literally believed in magic, he would have answered: No. "Magic, I felt, was no more than a first crude attempt at science, and it had now been superseded by science" (47). He continues:

"If I still accepted that view, I would not be writing this book. It now seems to me that the exact reverse is true. Magic was not the 'science' of the past. It is the science of the future. I believe that the human mind has reached a point in evolution where it is about to develop new powers—powers that would once have been considered magical." (47)

In the animal kingdom 'magical' powers (such as the homing instinct) are commonplace:

"Civilised man has forgotten about them because they are no longer necessary to his survival...*In fact, his survival depends upon 'forgetting' them.* High development of the instinctive levels is incompatible with the kind of concentration upon detail needed by civilised man." (53)

Wilson then recounts some incidents of premonition and telepathy in his personal life before outlining recorded cases of astral projection by John Cowper Powys and August Strindberg. This encourages Wilson to produce his own basic theory of the power of the human mind, introducing the important concept of 'Faculty X': "that latent power that human beings possess *to reach beyond the present*" (73):

"Faculty X is a sense of reality of other places and other times, and it is the possession of it—fragmentary and uncertain though it is—that distinguishes man from all other animals." (74)

He quotes examples of 'Faculty X' from Marcel Proust's autobiographical novel *À la Recherche du Temps Perdu* and Arnold Toynbee's *A Study of History*. These examples are of central importance to Wilson and will be referred to on numerous occasions in future works. 'Faculty X', Wilson insists, is an ordinary potentiality of consciousness, "...it is the key not only to so-called occult experience, but to the whole future evolution of the human race" (77). [Wilson considered this chapter important enough to include, in its entirety, in the self-edited collection *The*

Essential Colin Wilson (London: Harrap, 1985).]

Although he advised Wilson against writing such a book, Robert Graves seems to have contributed to it significantly. Part 1, Chapter 2: 'The Dark Side of the Moon', opens with a discussion between the two in which Graves asserts that 5 per cent of human beings have occult powers. This, of course, fascinates Wilson because "this is also the figure for the 'dominant minority' among human beings" (78). He feels that there are "many reasons for assuming that the two groups are identical" (78). But when he speaks of 'occult powers':

> "Graves's concern is less with witches or mystics than with poets, and his important work *The White Goddess* contains a theory of the nature of poetry that links it not only with the powers of the subconscious, but with traditional magical cults." (80)

Graves's idea is that there are two kinds of poetry: 'muse poetry' which he associates with the White Goddess of primitive lunar cults and 'Apollonian poetry' which attempts to banish lunar superstitions with pure solar reason. A poet, according to Wilson,

> "...is a person who is naturally mentally healthy and resilient, and who frequently experiences moments in [which] he is suddenly amazed and delighted to realise how *interesting* everything is.... He perceives that the world is rich with *meanings* that he would ordinarily overlook." (90)

He concludes that "Graves's 'lunar knowledge' is a reality—a reality of which poets become aware in moments of stillness" (91). And:

> "If we agree, then, that the 'muse poet' or the 'magician' is a

9

person whose mind is able to relax and grasp these deeper levels of meaning, we must also recognise that this is a two-way affair. The meaning is already there, external to his own mind, and his power to 'tune in' to it is only the beginning." (91)

We have now reached the essence of Wilson's philosophy: "The true 'direction' for consciousness lies in knowledge expansion, a wider and wider grasp of the relations of the actual world, to illuminate and supplement the 'lunar' insights of the subconscious." (97)

In order to prove that magical systems should not be relegated merely to the status of unsuccessful attempts at science, Wilson then devotes several pages to the *I Ching*, the Chinese Book of Changes, and concludes that its profoundest level of meaning is revealed when thinking about its symbols and ideas and not its power to foretell events:

"...the primary meaning of Yin is 'the cloudy, the overcast', while that of Yang is 'banners waving in the sun'. Could one devise more basic symbols of the central problem of human existence? Dullness and boredom versus the 'moments of insight'." (112)

In Chapter 3: 'The Poet as Occultist' Wilson states:

"The poet is a man in whom Faculty X is naturally more developed than in most people. Whilst most of us are ruthlessly 'cutting out' whole areas of perception, thus impoverishing our mental lives, the poet retains the faculty to be suddenly delighted by the sheer *reality* of the world 'out there'." (113)

This is made possible by their ability to concentrate and to still the mind—an ability most of us seem to have lost. He presents examples of telepathy, and the ability to project one's body elsewhere, recorded by August Strindberg, W.B. Yeats , A.L. Rowse, Louis Singer and others.

> "Art, music, philosophy, mysticism are all escape routes from the narrowness of everyday reality; but they all demand a large initial outlay of conscious effort; you have to sow before you can reap." (138)

In contrast, 'magic' or occultism is a simple direct method of escaping the narrowness of everydayness. The student of the occult looks within himself and "tries to reach down to his subliminal depths" (139). This, says Wilson, explains the importance of symbols, which have a power to appeal to the subconscious mind, and suggests there may be, as W.B. Yeats and Carl Jung asserted:

> "...a racial memory, which works in terms of symbols. This racial memory can be reached by 'hushing the unquiet mind', by reaching a certain depth of inner stillness where it becomes accessible to the limited individual memory." (133)

This brings Wilson back to the *I Ching* and initiates a discussion on the symbolism of the Tarot which contains "...shocks to jar the mind out of 'the triviality of everydayness', to induce concentration upon essentials" (149).

In Part Two, Chapter 1, 'The Evolution of Man', Wilson argues that life is a *purposive* process:

> "...science insists that the universe can be explained entirely in mechanical terms. If we can show this to be untrue, then we have provided the case for magic with the most solid kind of

foundation." (153)

When we make an effort, says Wilson, for example when learning to play a musical instrument, we slowly master the difficult process. If, however, we make no effort, then we barely achieve a coherent note:

> "As soon as I have observed the enormous difference between purposeful concentration and aimless drifting, I find it hard to believe that life has reached its present stage by drifting." (156)

Like Aldous Huxley, Wilson believes that if the mind has a 'subconscious' why should it not also have a 'super-conscious':

> "The powers of the 'superconscious' *are* within reach of the human will, provided it is fresh and alive. As soon as habit takes over—or what I have called elsewhere 'the robot'—they dwindle.... All disciplines aimed at increased use of these powers depend on a high level of optimism and will-drive.... A science—or knowledge system—which has no place for will or purpose is an obstruction to human evolution..." (180)

In Chapter 2, 'The Magic of Primitive Man', Wilson attempts to "outline the development of man's 'hidden powers' from the dawn of history to its 'Tower of Babel' period, the period of degeneration" (225). He presents evidence to suggest that Neanderthal and Cro-Magnon man were monotheistic, employing shamans as intermediaries who used intense concentration to achieve their aims. Then, as man's activities expanded so did the need for more gods:

> "All religion and occultism that spring from this intense concentration tend to be simple and mystical.... All the great

religions...are simple in this sense. In the hands of the common people—the non-religious 99 per cent—they soon lose this simplicity, this clarity of vision, and develop hoards of angels, gods and demons." (190-191)

In the next two chapters, Wilson considers the lives of some of the principal figures in the history of Western magic: "...the mage or adept is a fundamental human 'archetype': he symbolises man's evolutionary destiny" (228). The Magi, according to Wilson, derived their magic powers from 'positive consciousness' which he defines as:

"...a happy, open state of mind.... It is a sense of the marvellous *interestingness* of the world. We still use the word 'magic' in this sense—talking about 'the magic of summer nights', 'magic moments' and so on. This is not a misuse of language; that is what real magic is about." (239)

Sections are devoted to studies of the Magi, Orphism, the Essenes, the worship of the god Dionysius, alchemy, the Mystical Kabbalah and Gnosticism. The life and work of Pythagoras: "...the first 'great initiate' of recorded history" (248), Apollonius of Tyana, Albertus Magnus, Cornelius Agrippa, Nostradamus, Paracelsus and many others are considered.

At the beginning of Chapter 5, 'Adepts and Impostors', Wilson writes: "After the great sixteenth century there is a falling off in the quality of magic" (345). In it he considers the life and work of Dr. John Dee, Giacomo Casanova, Count Alessandro di Cagliostro, the Count of Saint-Germain and "the greatest occultist of the eighteenth century" (358) Emanuel Swedenborg.

In Chapter 6, 'The Nineteenth Century—Magic and Romanticism', we move into more familiar Wilson territory: "The romantics were driven by the spirit of magic, which is the evolutionary spirit of the human race" (420) but "wrapped in self-pity, they fail to stay the course" (422) ending in pessimism and despair: "with the exception of Goethe, the romantics seem unaware of that other form that ecstasy takes: the violent raging appetite for more life" (422). However, the romantic revival brought with it a revival of interest in magic: Madame Blavatsky and theosophy, W.B. Yeats, MacGregor Mathers and the Order of the Golden Dawn.

'The Beast Himself', Aleister Crowley, is the subject of Chapter 7. Wilson had previously based a character—Caradoc Cunningham—in his novel *Man Without A Shadow: the diary of an existentialist* (London: Arthur Barker, 1963) on Crowley and would go on to write a short biography *Aleister Crowley: the nature of the Beast* (Wellingborough: Aquarian Press, 1987). Chapter 8 is shared between Grigori Rasputin and the philosopher/mystic G.I. Gurdjieff. Wilson had already written a biography of Rasputin, *Rasputin and the Fall of the Romanovs* (London: Arthur Barker, 1964) and would write a novel based on his life, *The Magician From Siberia* (London: Robert Hale, 1988). But it is Gurdjieff whom he describes as "the most interesting of all magicians.... There can be no doubt that he achieved a large degree of Faculty X" (502). Again, he had written about Gurdjieff before, most notably in his *Outsider Cycle*** and would go on to write a short biography, *The War Against Sleep: the philosophy of Gurdjieff* (Wellingborough: Aquarian Press, 1980). Clearly Gurdjieff's message resonates with Wilson and, to a great extent, correlates with his own ideas about the inadequacy of human consciousness:

> "In the moments of 'higher consciousness' there is always a feeling of 'But *of course!*' Life is infinitely meaningful; its possibilities are suddenly endless, and 'normal consciousness' is seen as being no better than sleep. For, like sleep, it separates man from *reality*." (508)

Following his assessment of Gurdjieff, Wilson moves *The Occult* forward to its third and final part: 'Man's Latent Powers'. In Chapter 1 he presents a history of witchcraft including vampirism and lycanthropy. Chapter 2, 'The Realm of Spirits', contains accounts of spiritualism, ghosts, reincarnation and clairvoyance. In Chapter 3, 'Glimpses', he attempts "to suggest a general theory that might impose some order on the bewildering mass of occult phenomena already examined". (703). Wilson is convinced that, if can we learn to raise our consciousness above the 'everyday norm' we could re-acquaint ourselves with "various powers and faculties that at present are 'occult' (latent, hidden) and would discover that they are perfectly natural after all" (703). He recounts documented instances of telepathy, precognition and mystical experiences seeing these as evidence that we can, albeit fleetingly, tune into higher levels of consciousness. But why only 'fleetingly'?

"The answer is of fundamental importance. Because the 'muscles' that could hold it are flabby and undeveloped. We only make use of these muscles *involuntarily*, when suddenly stirred by beauty or a sense of crisis.... We possess the muscles for compressing consciousness and producing states of intensity, but we use them so seldom that we are hardly aware of their existence." (744).

Wilson asserts that the next stage in human evolution will be the "deliberate development of this 'muscle' of the will, and a corresponding development of the sense of meaning" (745). He goes on to explain how concentration can be employed to convulse the 'muscle'. Whilst listening to a favourite piece of music:

"Instead of allowing the aesthetic experience to operate upon passive sensibilities, I made an effort to accelerate the process by concentration.... I convulsed the muscle of concentration in an all-out effort, and the result was a glimpse of the kind of control over the body that *will* be possible at the next stage of human evolution." (748)

He later devised a method of inducing these 'peak' experiences using a concentration and relaxation method which he named the 'pen-trick'. This technique is explained in his book *Access to Inner Worlds* (London: Rider, 1983) and was taught, with a degree of success, to students at the Viittakivi Institute in Finland.

In conclusion Wilson writes:

"I do not regard myself as an 'occultist' because I am more interested in the mechanisms of everyday consciousness. In the past, man's chief characteristic has been his 'defeat proneness'; even the giants of the nineteenth century were inclined to believe that insanity is a valid refuge from the 'triviality of everydayness'. But the answer lies in understanding the mechanisms. Once they are understood, they can be altered to admit more reality. The operation requires concentration and precision, the virtues of a skilled watchmaker.

We return to the assertion of the opening chapter: man's future lies in the cultivation of 'Faculty X'." (763)

The critical response to this book was mostly good although, as with all of Wilson's work, responses were extreme: either enthusiastically positive or over-critical. But over all, reviews were lengthy and:

"...had a serious and respectful tone that I hadn't heard since *The Outsider.*... As if conveying the blessing of England's literary establishment, Cyril Connolly and Philip Toynbee... produced lengthy and thoughtful reviews.... Apparently all was forgiven." (Wilson (2); 18)

Alan Hull Walton, writing in *Books and Bookmen*, declared:

"...in an age of talented mediocrity, [Colin Wilson] is blessed with far more than talent—he is blessed with insight, sincerity, humility, an extraordinarily wide learning (comparable to that of the 'universal man' of the Renaissance), and also manifests something of the breadth of genius of a Goethe.... His new book... is by far and away his best work to date, and worthy to be placed on the same shelf alongside William James, F.W.H. Myers' *Human Personality...*, and Frazer's *Golden Bough*.... A review of a thousand words... cannot do justice to a book of this calibre.... *The Occult* is a valuable 'must' for anyone with the remotest interest in the future of civilised man." (Walton, 50-51)

However, E. Geoffrey Parrinder, in the *Times Literary Supplement*, was less effusive calling it a "hotchpotch of magic, witchcraft, spiritualism and the like", but admitting that:

"Mr. Wilson's theory that man has evolved so far outwardly that progress is in danger unless accompanied by inward development is a serious problem. [He should] take the thirty odd pages on Faculty X and develop a coherent theory without the occult allies.... Comparison with Frazer's *Golden Bough* is misconceived...." (Parrinder, 1471)

James Blish advised that "...anyone wishing to begin reading in this field might well begin with this book (which also contains a good bibliography)", with the proviso that "he retains a good grip on his scepticism". (Blish, 654)

In the U.S., Joyce Carol Oates praised the work as a "book of wonders", recommending it as: "one of those rich, strange, perplexing, infinitely surprising works that repay many readings. Though it contains a great deal of history it is really, like most of Colin Wilson's books, about the future." (Oates, 8-9) Clifford P. Bendau wrote:

"*The Occult* establishes that Wilson has the ability to research and interpret vast quantities of information. It is apparent that he is able to convey consistent and challenging ideas that prod those who are most comfortable with their established beliefs." (Bendau, 53)

"With the publication of *The Occult*", wrote Howard F. Dossor:

"...many readers believed that Wilson had redirected his interest to a new field.... Many thought he had abandoned his principles and settled for the acclaim of a more receptive press. For many, this suspicion was fuelled by his admission that he had been attracted to write the book as a means of solving his financial problems... [however] it is inconceivable that the author of *The Outsider Cycle* would not have proceeded to an investigation of the mysterious world that lies beyond the boundaries of our established sciences and our intellectual preconceptions. The very term *Outsider* implies an incapacity to remain restricted within such parameters. The Outsider is outside the prevailing myths of his age, no matter how respectable the form in which they present themselves." (Dossor, 178)

In a recent assessment of all three of Wilson's 'Occult Trilogy' books, Will Parker concludes:

"Through his reading of the occult and the paranormal—leavened with a reasonable knowledge of depth psychology and the neurosciences—Wilson offers a provisional set of working assumptions which point the way towards... promising new vistas of psychic evolution.... Wilson is at his best when bringing this esoteric conceptual framework to bear on his own special interest, the cultivation of the 'peak experience' as an antidote to the 'nausea' of modern man." (Parker, 25)

*All page references are from the Mayflower Books Ltd paperback edition of *The Occult*. St Albans: Mayflower Books Ltd., 1973 (1976 reprint).

** The *Outsider Cycle* is as follows:
The Outsider (1956)
Religion and the Rebel (1957)
The Age of Defeat (*The Stature of Man* in the U.S.) (1959)
The Strength to Dream: literature and the imagination (1962)
Origins of the Sexual Impulse (1963)
Beyond the Outsider: the philosophy of the future (1965)
Introduction to the New Existentialism (1966)

References:

Bendau, Clifford P. *Colin Wilson: the Outsider and beyond*. San Bernardino: The Borgo Press, 1979.

Blish, James. 'Eclectic Occultism' in *The Spectator* 227, (Nov.6, 1971) p. 654.

Dossor, Howard F. *Colin Wilson: the man and his mind*. Shaftesbury, Dorset: Element Books, 1990.

Oates, Joyce Carol. Review of *The Occult* in *The American Poetry Journal* II (January/February, 1973), p. 8-9.

Parker, Will. 'Colin Wilson on the Occult' in *The Gnostic*, Issue 2 (Autumn 2009), p. 17-26.

Parrinder, E. Geoffrey. 'What we need is Faculty X', *Times Literary Supplement* (Nov. 26, 1971), p. 1471.

Walton, Alan Hull. 'Wilson's occult' in *Books and Bookmen*, 17, (Dec. 1971), p. 50-51.

Wilson, Colin (1). New Introduction to *The Occult*. London:

Watkins Publishing, 2003.

Wilson, Colin (2). 'Introduction: *The Outsider*, twenty years on' in *The Outsider*. London: Pan (Picador) Books, 1978.

Bibliographical details:

The Occult.

a. London: Hodder & Stoughton, 1971, 601 p., cloth.

b. New York: Random House, 1971, 603 p., cloth.

c. New York: Random House, 1972?, 603 p., cloth, [book club edition].

d. St. Albans: Mayflower, 1973, 795 p., paper.

e. as: *The Occult: A History*. New York: Vintage Books, 1973, 601 p., paper.

f. as: *L'Occulte*. Paris: Albin Michel, 1973, 425 p., paper. Translated by Robert Genin. [French]

g. as: *Lo Oculto: La Facultad X del Hombre*. Barcelona: Editorial Noguer, 1974, 476 p., cloth. Translated by Carmen Criado. [Spanish]

h. as: *L'Occulto*. Roma: Astrolabio, 1975, 623 p., cloth (?). Translated by Paolo Valli. [Italian]

i. as: *Den Hemmelighedsfulde Videnskab*. Viby: Strube, 1978, 372 p., cloth (?). Translated by Benjamin Saxe. [Danish]

j. London: Granada, 1979, 795 p., paper.

k. as: *O Oculto*. Rio de Janeiro: Livraria Francisco Alves Editora, 1981, 2v., vol. 1: 273 p., vol. 2: 248 p., paper. Translated by Aldo Bocchini Netto. [Portuguese]

l. as: *Das Okkulte*. Berlin: Marz, 1982, ? p., cloth (?). [German]

m. as: *Okaruto*. Tokyo: Shinchosha, n.d., 2 v., cloth (?). Translated by Yasuo Nakamura. [Japanese]

n. as: *Het Occulte*. Deventer: Ankh-Hermes, n.d., 335 p., cloth (?). Translated by Margot Bakker. [Dutch]

o. as: *L'Occulte*. Lausanne: Ex Libris, n.d., 427 p., cloth (?). Translated by Robert Genin. [French]

p. as: "Magic—the Science of the Future *(The Occult)*" in *The Essential Colin Wilson*. London: Harrap, 1985, cloth, p. 108-129. A reprint of a section from this volume.

q. [Japanese edition] Tokyo: Hirakawa Shuppan Ltd., 1985, 643 p., cloth. [ISBN: 4-89203-101-1]

r. as: *The Occult: a history*. New York: Barnes & Noble, 1995, 603 p., cloth.

s. as: *The Occult: the ultimate book for those who would walk with the Gods*. London: Watkins Publishing, 2003, [xli, 753 p.] xli, 795 p., paper. [Includes a new 4-page Introduction by Wilson]

t. as: *Ocultismul*. Bucharest: Pro Editura si Tipografie, n.d., 663 p., paper. Translated by Laura Chivu. ISBN: 978-973-145-074-2. [Romanian]

u. as: *Das Okkulte*. Köln: Parkland Verlag, 2004, 858 p., cloth. Trans. By Helma Schleif & Nils Thomas Lindquist. [German]

Dedication: "For Robert Graves."

ANALYTICAL TABLE OF CONTENTS:

Preface: Faculty X. Introduction. "Unseen forces"; The need for an occult revival; The attitude of science; Cybernetics: the intelligent universe; Wilson's change of attitude towards occultism.

PART ONE: A Survey of the Subject. Chapter One: Magic—the Science of the Future. P.D. Ouspensky and "infinitely remote horizons"; Homing instinct; Dowsing; Synchronicity; Precognition; Telepathy; Evil eye; John Cowper Powys' spectre; Faculty X; Arnold Toynbee's experience. Chapter Two: The Dark Side of the Moon. The dominant 5%; Robert Graves and *The White Goddess*; Man's "lunar powers"; Hypertension; *I Ching*; Taoism and Zen. Chapter Three: The Poet as Occultist. Louis Singer and paranormal phenomena; A. L. Rowse's telepathy; W.B. Yeats' theory of symbols; Yeats and *A Vision*; The tarot.

PART TWO: A History of Magic. Chapter One: The Evolution of Man. H.G. Wells and evolution; Life—accidental or purposive?; J.B. Rhine's PK tests; Peak experiences; Contemplative objectivity; Failure of psychedelic drugs; Use of sex; The superconscious. Chapter Two: The Magic of Primitive Man. Shamanism; The dawn of magic; Man becomes a city-dweller; The rise of his sexual obsession; *The Epic of Gilgamesh;* Atlantis; Egyptian religion and magic. Chapter Three: Adepts and Initiates. Thaumaturgy; "Positive consciousness"; Ancient Greece; The Essenes; Orphism and the worship of Dionysus; Pythagoras; Apollonius of Tyana; Dowsing. Chapter Four: The World of the Kabbalists. Gnosticism; *The Kabbalah;* Simon Magus; Early Christianity; Joseph of Copertino, the flying monk; Possessed nuns; Benvenuto Cellini; Dionysius the Areopagite; Albertus Magnus; Cornelius Agrippa; Paracelsus; Alchemy; Astrology; Nostradamus and his prediction of the French Revolution. Chapter Five: Adepts and Impostors. John Dee; Emanuel Swedenborg; Anton Mesmer; Casanova; Cagliostro; The Count of Saint-Germain. Chapter Six: The Nineteenth Century—magic and romanticism. Saint-Martin; Eliphaz Levi; The Fox sisters; Madame Blavatsky and the Theosophical Society; W.B. Yeats, Mathers, and the Order of the Golden Dawn. Chapter Seven: The Beast Himself. Crowley's childhood; His sexual obsession; Magic; Marriage; The abbey of Theleme; His death. Chapter Eight: Two Russian Mages. Gregory Rasputin; His thaumaturgie powers; Success at court; Enemies; His Murder; Georges Gurdjieff; His childhood; Travels; His basic ideas; "disciples," particularly P.D. Ouspensky and J.G. Bennett; Subud.

PART THREE: Man's Latent Powers. Chapter One: Witchcraft and Lycanthropy. Origins of European witchcraft; Catharism; The spread of the witch-craze; Exorcism of nuns; Matthew Hopkins, the witch-finder general; Why the witchcraft craze died out; The rise of the novel; Valéry Briussov's *The Fiery Angel;* Vampirism and lycanthropy: their sexual basis; The case of Sally

Beauchamp; Cases of vampirism; The witchcraft revival. Chapter Two: The Realm of the Spirits. Daniel Dunglas Home; C.G. Jung and the unconscious; Aldous Huxley and J.B. Rhine; Founding of the Society for Psychical Research; Harry Price; Poltergeists; Spontaneous combustion; Ted Serios; Reincarnation; Arthur Guirdham; UFOs; The Tunguska explosion; Jack Schwarz. Chapter Three: Glimpses. The "vital force" and animal magnetism; Reichenbach's "odic force"; Wilhelm Reich; Precognition; J.B. Priestley; J.W. Dunne; Eternal recurrence; Experiences of mystical consciousness; The seventh degree of concentration; The pineal eye; Serotonin, the Faculty X hormone; Development of life on Earth; The need for challenge and crisis. "Man's future lies in the cultivation of Faculty X." Bibliography. Index.

COMMENTS:

Wilson's most important work since the Outsider Cycle. Faculty X, "the latent power that human beings possess to reach beyond the present," is the thread that links together this massive peregrination of the occult. Viewed simply as a reference source for its subject, it rates alongside some of the classics in the field. But *The Occult* goes further than merely presenting supernatural "evidence." Part Three, Chapter Three, "Glimpses," points the way to a new stage in the evolution of mankind, presented with Wilson's usual optimism and zeal.

The latest Watkins paperback has a new 4-page Introduction by Wilson in which he describes how the success of the book pushed him back onto the bestseller lists after an absence of 15 years, adding: "The English paperback came out in a large, grass-green volume, with some nonsensical quote about it being 'a book for those who would walk with the gods.'" Interestingly, this new edition uses that quote as its sub-title!

The cloth editions contain a set of black-and-white plates between pages 304-305.

SECONDARY SOURCES AND REVIEWS:

1. Adams, Phoebe. *Atlantic* 229 (Jan., 1972): 96.
2. Bendau, p. 52-53.
3. Bergström—mentioned throughout.
4. *Book Review Digest* (Annual 1972): 1400.
5. *Booklist* 68 (Feb. 15, 1972): 470.
6. *Books & Bookmen* 20 (Jan., 1975): 81.
7. Brogan, Diarmuid. *Yorkshire Post* (Oct. 9, 1971): nk.
8. Byatt, A.S. *Times* (Oct. 21, 1971): 12.
9. Celebration: Chapter 20.
10. *Choice* 9 (Apr., 1972): 200.
11. Clare, John. "Colin Wilson Tackles 'Faculty X,' So Fateful for Man," in *Times* (Oct. 20, 1971): 4.
12. Dossor: Chapter 6.
13. *Economist* 241 (Oct. 6, 1971): R22.
14. Galbreath, R. *American Society of Psychical Research Journal* 69 (Jan., 1975): 84-91.
15. *Guardian Weekly* 105 (Dec. 16, 1971): 22.
16. *Kirkus Reviews* 39 (Sept. 1, 1971): 1005.
17. *Life* 71 (Dec. 31, 1971): 25.
18. Lima, Robert. *Saturday Review of Literature* 55 (Jan. 15, 1972): 48.
19. Needleman, Jacob. *Commonweal* 96 (Apr. 21, 1973): 173.
20. Oates, Joyce Carol. *American Poetry Review* 2 (Jan./Feb., 1973): 8-9.
21. *Observer* (Oct. 17, 1971): 33.
22. *Publishers Weekly* 200 (Sept. 27, 1971): 64.
23. *Publishers Weekly* 203 (Jan. 8, 1973): 66.
24. Rees, Gorownwy. "Gurus Galore." *Encounter* 39 (Aug., 1972): 56-58.
25. Blish, James "Eclectic Occultism" in *Spectator* 227 (Nov. 6, 1971): 654.
26. Stanford, Derek. *Scotsman* (Oct. 9, 1971): nk.
27. Parrinder, E. Geoffrey "What we need is Faculty X" in

Times Literary Supplement (Nov. 26, 1971): 1471.

28. Walton, Alan Hull. "Wilson's Occult." *Books & Bookmen* 17 (Dec, 1971): 50-51. (Reprinted Celebration, Chapter 20.)

29. Weigel, p. 124-126.

30. West, R.H. *Review of Politics* 37 (Oct., 1975): 547-556.

31. Payne, Paddy. "An Eye to the Future" (Nov. 13, 1971): 10.

32. Stanley: *Literary Encyclopedia* http://www.litencyc.com/

Book 2: *Mysteries: an investigation into the occult, the paranormal and the supernatural*

❀

Mysteries, with its long sub-title, the second book in Wilson's 'Occult Trilogy' (commencing with *The Occult* (1971) and concluding with *Beyond the Occult* (1988)), was published in the UK by Hodder & Stoughton in September 1978 and by G.P. Putnam's Sons in the US shortly afterwards. *The Occult*, a book of over 600 pages, Wilson's first commissioned work, was so successful that the publishers requested a sequel. He responded with a book of even greater length which, like its predecessor, was divided into three parts preceded by an Introduction.

This Introduction, 'The Ladder of Selves', contains some important insights and, indeed, was included by Wilson in *The Essential Colin Wilson* (London: Harrap, 1985) and also re-issued as an e-book *The Ladder of Selves* and *The Search for Power Consciousness* (Berkeley, CA: Maurice Bassett) in 2002. It commences with Wilson recounting a series of 'panic attacks' that he suffered in the mid-1970s and the steps he took to overcome them, providing yet another example of Wilson's use of personal experience to elucidate his ideas:

> 'The panic...was caused by a lower level of my being, an incompetent and childish 'me'. As long as I identified with this 'me', I was in danger. But the rising tension could always be countered by *waking myself up fully* and calling upon a more purposive 'me'. It was like a schoolmistress walking into a room of squabbling children and clapping her hands. The chaos would subside instantly....' (28)*

Accessing this higher self can give us the means of controlling the dozens of 'I's' scattered inside us, at various levels, like a ladder. "All forms of purposive activity evoke a higher 'I'" (28), writes Wilson, and can aid our ascent:

"But reflecting on this image, it struck me that the ladder...is shaped like a triangle, so that the higher rungs are shorter than the lower ones. When I move up the ladder, I experience a sense of concentration and control. When I move down—through depression or fatigue—my being seems to become diffused...and I begin to feel at the mercy of the world around me." (36)

Wilson uses this theory to 'explain' certain occult phenomena and to attack the problem of absurdity or meaninglessness:

The world around us seethes with endless activity, and this normally strikes us as quite reasonable. But there are certain moments of fatigue or depression when this meaning seems to crack under us.... According to the ladder-of-selves theory, this is precisely what one would expect in a state of low inner-pressure. But it is *not* an inescapable part of the human condition.... In moments of intensity, of excitement, of creativity, I move up the ladder and instantly become aware that the meaninglessness was an illusion...." (44)

Part One introduces the work of the British archaeologist and parapsychologist T. C. Lethbridge: "The only investigator of the twentieth century who has produced a comprehensive and convincing theory of the paranormal" (46), to a wider audience. According to Wilson, Lethbridge's books fall into four groups:

"...books on archaeology and primitive religion, and the books on pendulums and related matters. *Legend of the Sons of God* [1972] ...about visitors from other worlds and the magnetic forces of the earth, belongs in a group on its own. The same is true of...*The Power of the Pendulum* [1976] in which he seemed about to embark on a new line of enquiry about dreams and the nature of time." (76)

All of these aspects of Lethbridge's work are considered in Part One of *Mysteries*. The contributions of other researchers, where relevant, are brought into the mix: Alfred Watkins, John Michell, Guy Underwood, Robert [Allan] Monroe, J. W. Dunne and J. B. Priestley among others. Wilson applies his 'ladder of selves' theory to explain the phenomenon of dowsing:

> "...there can be no doubt that what we accept as everyday consciousness is thoroughly sub-normal. In which case, it seems a fair guess that such faculties as dowsing, second-sight, precognition and divination may simply be latent in some higher level...." (75)

Lethbridge was a natural dowser, who no doubt found this skill useful when excavating archaeological sites. But when someone suggested that, instead of a hazel twig, he should use a pendulum, he began, in his later years, a series of pioneering experiments using pendulums of varying lengths (or 'rates') to divine, at first, various metals and then all manner of objects. His experiments also revealed that these objects all have vibrational 'fields' surrounding them, the radius being that of the 'rate' for the object. Extending this 'field theory' to ghost sightings, "...Lethbridge [was] the first to speculate on whether hauntings may not be connected with the 'field' of water" (64).

> "All his books are pervaded by an underlying feeling of excitement. He believed that he was on the point of some important breakthrough...basically a feeling that the answer lies somehow in *rates of vibration* [and] if matter can be explained in terms of vibrations, then the same thing

probably applies to the world of 'paranormal' phenomena....
What really excited him was that his own investigations
seemed to be somehow connecting up with those of modern
physics. Everything in the universe seemed to have a 'rate'—
just as the elements all have their atomic weights." (170-171)

In Part 2, Chapter 1: 'The Curious History of Human Stupidity',
Wilson asserts that:

"Human beings possess a powerful stabilising mechanism
which operates on the psychological as well as the physical
level.... A person who feels deeply insecure is afraid to begin
living. *That* is why we tend to ignore things that upset our
basic sense of normality—or to forget them as quickly as
possible...." (202)

But the evidence for the existence of paranormal phenomena is
such that we need to keep an open mind for fear of taking a
similar stance to the clergy against early scientists and, latterly,
scientists against theologians and philosophers. Wilson outlines
the danger and absurdity of the closed mind and argues:

"Obviously neither science nor religion possesses a monopoly
on truth. Ideally science is the impersonal pursuit of truth; but
then, so is religion—as all the saints and mystics have recog-
nised. And to pursue truth requires some of the qualities of a
saint or mystic. Ordinary human beings are too easily swayed
by the appetite for power and recognition and self-esteem."
(197)

He sees investigators like Lethbridge and the rigidly methodical
collector of anomalous phenomena Charles Hoy Fort as "tak[ing]
pleasure in the fact that the world is bursting with anomalies"
(203).

"The problem is to strike a balance between the two extremes. We need a world with enough strangeness and 'newness' to keep us awake but not enough to produce a feeling of insecurity.... Most scientists seem to have a strong compulsion to cling to their old paradigms." (203)

[Taking up the 'Fortean' mantle, Wilson himself went on to edit the part-work *The Unexplained* (London: Orbis Publishing Co., 1980-83) and, with his son Damon, *The Encyclopedia of Unsolved Mysteries* (London: Harrap, 1987). He has also spoken at many of the *FortFest* Conventions around the world. This open-mindedness has left him open to accusations of gullibility by academics and sceptics but his stance is entirely consistent with his conviction that all human beings possess latent 'occult' powers.]

Chapter 2 'How Many Me's Are There?' examines the phenomenon of multiple personality, quoting cases recorded by Carl Jung and Pierre Janet and those of the remarkable Christine Beauchamp, Doris Fischer (who had five distinctive personalities) and Sybil Dorsett (sixteen!). To help explain this phenomenon, Wilson uses Janet's theory (and that of the philosopher and scientist Michael Polanyi) that human consciousness has a hierarchy of levels and that our lives evolve as we climb to higher levels, successfully integrating each stage as we progress. In all cases of multiple personality it appears that the subject's progress had become arrested: "they had ceased to climb" (229), releasing a number of unfulfilled personalities:

"We can think of a human being as a small garden containing a number of seeds at various depths. If all goes well, and the human being strives for self-actualisation...then the 'seeds' awaken one by one, and quietly integrate with those that have already started to germinate. But if the human being becomes severely discouraged...the whole personality becomes static.

The seeds start to germinate, put out a few buds, then 'freeze'. (232)

At the end of the chapter Wilson reminds us that, although we are certainly not all multiple personality cases, we are, however, all characterised by a tendency to 'duality':

"No matter how involved...in an emotion or enthusiasm, a part of the ego remains detached, uninvolved.... We are all 'divided' from the moment of birth; it is a condition of our evolution.

These recognitions are not a discovery of modern 'depth psychology'. They are part of an esoteric tradition that is older than civilisation. Oddly enough, its name is magic." (234)

In the following chapters Wilson concerns himself with the power of the will allied to the imagination, particularly with regard to making magic work. Imagination is "...the power to get back to reality, to re-focus our true values, to combat the curious erosion of our vitality" (266-7). He considers the invention of the novel (which he argues dates from 1740 with the publication of Samuel Richardson's *Pamela*) "one of the most remarkable events in human cultural history" (255). Richardson "taught the middle-classes the use of the imagination" (256) and inspired "the expanding revolution of the human spirit that we call roman-ticism" (256).

He discusses also the "old magical art of memory" (254) and the way that our accumulated knowledge can enhance our experience of 'Faculty X' ["that latent power that human beings possess *to reach beyond the present*" (Wilson (1), 73)]:

"...the meaning-content of such an experience depends on the amount we know. For an ignoramus, Faculty X would merely be a pleasant sense that 'all is well'....For a philosopher, it could be an insight into the meaning of human existence." (251)

Dreams, visions, revelations, alchemy, Cabbalism, possession, poltergeists, reincarnation and many other topics are dealt with in this rich section of the book. But it is when Wilson considers Jung's collective unconscious, in the chapter entitled 'The Rediscovery of Magic', that he introduces us to the potentially useful concept of 'gliding', a method of establishing contact with the unconscious: "[Gliding is] probably the simplest and most accessible to the ordinary person, and there are few people unlucky enough never to have experienced it" (316):

"It happens frequently when you relax in front of the fire and pour yourself a drink.... It happens to children at Christmas time...when a whole range of reinforced stimuli...build up a mood of intensity and delight.... In all cases it is easy to see how the effect works. The mind relaxes into a state [of] 'pleasant expectancy'. Among the normal anxieties and tensions of modern life, we grow accustomed to a fairly constant flow of negative stimuli, and we finally slip into a state of negative expectation.... When 'pleasant expectancy' is slightly higher than usual, we can gradually de-condition ourselves out of the negative responses.... A person who has unusually strong reasons for feeling happiness...may quickly reach the normal 'ceiling' for positive response and pass straight through it into a 'floating' state of ecstasy. Such states...can produce an effect of stunning paradox and overwhelming joy that can produce floods of tears or an ecstatic sense of the goodness of the universe." (316-7)

However, instead of trying to grasp and analyse these states, most of us fail to learn from our experiences of a more relaxed consciousness. In the following chapter, 'Revelations', Wilson looks at some of those who have learned and progressed further.

Wilson has often been criticised for his interest in the occult. In this book he argues that "the paranormal often leads directly to questions of philosophy" (504). However, many casual readers of his earlier work failed to see the connection between this and his 'new existentialism'. Towards the end of this section, in the chapter entitled 'Powers of Evil?' Wilson explains the development of his own field of interest from 'outsiderism' to the paranormal:

> "The 'outsider' is aware of being trapped in his own narrow personality, and he suffers from a sense of suffocation.... But the 'outsider' suffers so much because he has had moments in which he experienced an intoxicating sense of freedom, in which his consciousness seemed somehow enlarged.... The great romantics, from Rousseau to T. E. Lawrence, were all driven by this desire to escape from 'themselves' and explore the realms of freedom." (492)

But exploring the 'realms of freedom' is a task that has preoccupied philosophers throughout time and Wilson sees psychics, dowsers, clairvoyants etc as somehow having occasional access to these realms even if some of their evidence is not always reliable.

In the final part of *Mysteries*, Wilson turns his attention to evolution and argues that mental evolution is a basic law of the universe: "It is as if a higher level of consciousness [is] trying to persuade us to bring it into actuality" (505). He feels that there is "something unsatisfactory about the Darwinian theory of evolution" (507) and goes on to consider others, in particular Stan Gooch's theory of evolution through the inner conflict between man's new and old brains, the cerebrum and the cerebellum, and

Charlotte Bach's [i.e. Karoly Hajdu] idea of sexual aberration driving evolution.

[Students wishing to know more about the work of Charlotte Bach are referred to Wilson's 1988 book *The Misfits: a Study of Sexual Outsiders*, (London: Grafton Books).]

But there is an obstacle to evolution and it is 'the robot', Wilson's name for the mental servant that we have developed to perform automatic tasks for us: "man has allowed himself...to become too dependent on the 'robot', until low-consciousness has become part of our human heritage" (526).

"The odd thing is that the brain circuits that produce wider consciousness are not waiting to evolve; they are already there.... The strange implication seems to be that there *was* a time when we made fuller use of them, and that our capacities have been atrophied since those days." (525)

Wilson sees this as something equivalent to the Fall in Genesis:

"Like the Original Sin of Genesis, our low-pressure consciousness can be held responsible for most of our major defects. It produces a kind of nagging hunger for excitement that leads to all kinds of irrational behaviour. This is why gamblers gamble, sex maniacs commit rape...why men become alcoholics and drug addicts. It also explains why we are so prone to outbreaks of criminality and mass destruction. Violence and pain are preferable to boredom and frustration." (526)

So is there a way forward for mankind? The 'robot' is essential to all life, yet it is also a jailer. As always, Wilson, the consummate optimist, says yes. We need to "shake the mind awake" (527). Discomfort can do this but "a sense of purpose can do it more positively and effectively" (527). We must learn from the sense of freedom we experience in moments of excitement or happiness. An emergency can concentrate the mind and call up vital reserves of energy and we should be able to call upon these reserves whenever we please by adopting meditative techniques, or indeed Wilson's 'gliding' or by making "sudden convulsive efforts of concentration" (529). Persisting with these disciplines, Wilson asserts, produces a cumulative effect that will provide us with greater control over our inner freedom and expand our consciousness.

In the next chapter, 'Messages from Space and Time', Wilson looks at the evidence for alien intervention in human evolution. He considers the extra-terrestrial claims of Dr Andrija Puharich, Uri Geller, John Keel, F. W. Holiday (1920-1979) and others but retains an open mind:

> "All these speculations fail to suggest a definite answer to the problem of UFOs.... We cannot draw a line between the latent powers of the human mind, and the invisible powers that may exist around us in the universe.... [There is] an uncertainty principle in paranormal phenomena. They may be 'genuine' yet still not what they seem." (562)

Wilson then reminds us of the central theme of his book: that man has many levels or 'selves':

> "The being who looks out of my eyes is not 'me' at all. He is an impostor. The real 'me' is up there, beyond my present consciousness. He knows things that 'I' do not know. Consequently he can plan things that are beyond my under-standing.
>
> This recognition could provide the basic hypothesis needed if we are to understand the nature and purpose of UFOs." (564)

In the next chapter: 'The Mechanisms of Enlightenment' he looks more closely at the structure of the ladder of selves "and the actual mechanism by which we move up or down". (565) He provides examples of men and women who have moved up the ladder and assures us that we all have the capacity to do so. This does, however, require effort and the majority of us prefer not to be bothered. With one of his favourite analogies, Wilson describes human beings as like "grandfather clock[s] driven by watch spring[s]" (586). The villain of the piece is 'the robot', who does much of our living for us, with the result that our consciousness remains perpetually low unless galvanised by some external crisis. He reminds us that we have to *pay* attention:

> "What is wrong with most of our experience is that, instead of paying an honest price, we are always trying to cheat. We try to have the experience with the minimum of attention; but we only get out of it exactly as much as we put in...." (587)

The secret is to realise that consciousness is *intentional* [i.e. when we look at something we actually fire our attention at it like an archer firing an arrow at a target] and Wilson suggests a simple exercise to enable us to pour more intentionality into our perception: stare at an object "and then concentrate all your attention, as if looking at it closely was a matter of life and death. The result...is a sudden deepening of meaning" (590). Doing this regularly can have the effect of "strengthening the 'muscle' with which we focus reality" (590):

> "What we are speaking about...is Faculty X...the ability to grasp the reality not simply of *other* times and places, but of the present moment as well. And this observation makes us aware of the basic problem. As we merely look around us at ordinary objects, we are not seeing 'reality'; only a kind of shadowy, symbolic reality.... It is necessary to grasp clearly

that ordinary perception is little better than a fever, in which all objects are slightly unreal." (590)

Not only is consciousness intentional, it is also *relational* "as if everything I look at has *invisible threads* running from it to all the surrounding objects" (593). When consciousness is doing its proper work it is as if the archer fires a *shower* of arrows simultaneously. For Wilson "the recognition that consciousness is 'relational' as well as intentional has an important corollary: perception *itself is a creative act*...and like all other forms of creation, it yields results in proportion to the effort" (593-4). He argues that what we call 'mystical experience' is really simply 'wider relational consciousness' and that "once this is understood, the distinction between mysticism and common sense, between the normal and the paranormal, begins to dissolve" (594).

In the final chapter, 'Other Dimensions', Wilson, whilst admitting that "the whole realm of the paranormal seems to be so mad and *disconnected*" (611) sums up and restates his theory:

"In this book I have attempted to show that one simple hypothesis can bring a certain amount of order into the confusion: the notion that the mind of man possesses many levels. We are familiar enough with the notion of unconscious levels, and the fact that such functions as digestion and body temperature operate on these levels. It is no more difficult to grasp the proposition that 'paranormal powers' could also operate on other levels of consciousness. The most controversial consequence of this assumption is that these powers are not *waiting* to evolve; they are already fully evolved, and are simply waiting for us to achieve a level at which we can make use of them..." (611)

He feels strongly that "...human consciousness is developing towards a new recognition: that the way ahead lies through more consciousness, not less." (629)

As with all of Wilson's books post-*The Outsider*, reviews were extreme. Alan Hull Walton, in *Books and Bookmen*, described it as Wilson's "magnum opus" and could scarcely contain his admiration for the author:

> "The detail and wide range of the book...defies analysis in these few pages.... There is...only a single word which adequately sums up the qualities of this enormous opus of over 260,000 words—already a 'classic' in its own right—and that word is *superlative*.... [I]t reflects an almost superhuman amount of research and magically ruminative thought, both of which belong to that quality defined as 'genius'." (Walton 41, 43)

Norris Merchant, of *The Christian Century*, is not so impressed, accusing Wilson of becoming "fashionably glib":

> "But however shallow, Wilson is still erudite.... Which is to say that although *this* Colin Wilson differs from the original model of 1956, having become more dashing but with a decidedly lowered spiritual temperature as he speeds through his paraphrasing, he is an extremely useful version of himself.
>
> By reading Wilson, one becomes superficially up-to-date in every scrap of avant-garde research or speculation into "mysteries", whether of dowsing, UFOs or the sexual fantasias of Dr. Charlotte Bach." (Merchant, 712-3)

Oddly, Merchant makes no reference to the main theme of the book: Wilson's 'ladder of selves' theory. Howard F. Dossor feels that this theory:

"...has profound implications for a philosophy of human existence. It provides a possible explanation for the sense of meaninglessness which is endemic within twentieth century man. Surrounded by a panorama of astonishing variety and richness, we live on the bottom rung of the ladder so that our view is restricted. Inevitably we become bored with the puny environment our vision extends to, like a child whose sense of wonder at a particular toy gradually drains away as the hours pass. But once we begin to ascend the ladder, the sense of meaning expands and our sense of self expands with it." (Dossor, 195)

Professor Stanley Krippner, in his essay on *Mysteries* for the festschrift *Around the Outsider*, offers an interesting explanation for what he calls "Wilson's mixture of skepticism and credulity" (Krippner, 163). He describes Wilson as a 'particular humanist', one who "holds that science does not necessarily occupy a privileged position but may be subordinate to literature, art, music, or even mysticism in approaching certain questions..." (Krippner, 165) and concludes:

"If scientifically-orientated readers can accept the orientation of *Mysteries* as that of a particular humanist, they can take issue with specific parts of the book where the evidence is less than what they might find persuasive. But at the same time they can derive both enjoyment and insight from what the rest of this incredible treatise has to offer regarding human potential and its manifestations." (Krippner, 171)

*All quotes taken from the 1979 Panther [London: Granada Publishing] paperback edition of *Mysteries*.

References:

Dossor, Howard F. *Colin Wilson: the man and his mind.* Shaftesbury, Dorset: Element Books, 1990.

Krippner, Stanley, 'A Retrospective look at *Mysteries* from the perspective of parapsychology' in Stanley, Colin (ed.) *Around the Outsider*. Winchester: O-Books, 2011, p. 160-173.

Merchant, Norris, 'Insider' in *The Christian Century* 96 (July 4-11, 1979): 712-713.

Walton, Alan Hull, 'Colin Wilson's Magnum Opus' in *Books and Bookmen*, (March 1979): 41-43 (reprinted in Stanley, Colin (ed.): *Colin Wilson, a Celebration*. London: Cecil Woolf, 1988, p. 130-136).

Wilson, Colin (1) *The Occult*. London: Mayflower Books, 1973.

Bibliographical details:

Mysteries: An Investigation into the Occult, the Paranormal, and the Supernatural.

a. London: Hodder and Stoughton, 1978, 667 p., cloth.

b. New York: G. P. Putnam's Sons, 1978, 667 p., cloth, [no sub title].

c. New York: A Paragon Book, G.P. Putnam's Sons, 1980, 688 p., paper, [no subtitle].

d. London, New York: Granada, Panther Books, 1980, 667 p., paper.

e. [Japanese edition] Tokyo: Kousakusha Workshop, nd., 676 p., cloth. Translated by Kazuhisa Takahashi, Akimasa Minamitani and Makoto Takahashi.

f. as: "The Ladder of Selves *(Mysteries),*" in *The Essential Colin Wilson*. London: Harrap, 1985, cloth, p. 130-149. A reprint of a section from this volume.

g. London: Watkins Publishing, 2006, [xxvi, 644p] xxvi, 667 p., paper. [Contains a new 4-page Introduction by Wilson]

h. as: *The Ladder of Selves and The Search for Power*

Consciousness. Berkeley,CA: Maurice Bassett, 2002, e-book reprint of two chapters from this volume

Dedication: "For Eddie Campbell, with affection."

ANALYTICAL TABLE OF CONTENTS:

Introduction: The Ladder of Selves. Wilson and "panic attacks"; The "schoolmistress effect"; Gurdjieff's power to transfer energy; The ladder of selves and paranormal phenomena; "All is well" feeling; Attempt at a comprehensive theory of the occult.

PART ONE. Chapter One: Ghosts, Ghouls, and Pendulums. Tom Lethbridge and dowsing; How to use the pendulum; Ghouls; Lethbridge's "field" theory of ghosts and ghouls; Sir Oliver Lodge's "tape recording" theory; Electrical theory of the paranormal; The pendulum and the afterlife; Summary of Lethbridge's work. Chapter Two: Giants and Witches. Lethbridge and the Wandlebury Camp giant; Margaret Murray; Silbury Hill: Michael Dames' theory; The "old religion" in Cornwall; Are the stone megaliths storage batteries? Chapter Three: The path of the dragon. Lethbridge and Erich von Däniken; The latter's inaccuracies; Stonehenge; Robert Temple's *Sirius Mystery*; Alfred Watkins and ley lines; Guy Underwood; John Michell; The earth as a living being; Poltergeists and ley lines; More about Stonehenge: the theories of Alexander Thorn and Gerald Hawkins. Chapter Four: The Timeless Zone. Dreams of the future; Lethbridge and J. W. Dunne; Levels of sleep; Rapid eye movements; Robert Monroe's out-of-body experiences and precognitive dreams; Can electrical fields aid telepathy?; W. E. Boyd and Peter Maddock.

PART TWO. Chapter One: The Curious History of Human Stupidity. Van Vogt's "right man" theory; Science versus occultism and theology; Persecution of Giordano Bruno, Galileo, etc.; The evolution controversy: Cuvier, Lamarck, Darwin, etc.; Charles Fort and his ideas. Chapter Two: How Many Me's are

There? Dual personality; Jung's first case; His poltergeistexperiences; Multiple personality: Mary Reynolds, Doris Fischer, etc.; Wilder Penfield's discovery of "memory playback"; Pierre Janet and the nine levels of consciousness; The inhibition of personality. Chapter Three: In Search of Faculty X. Levitation; The control of psi-power; Magic; Importance of will and imagination; Visualization; What is imagination?; Bruno on man's godlike powers; Modern pessimism; Consciousness isintentional. Chapter Four: The Rediscovery of Magic. Jung and the collective unconscious; John Layard; Jung's technique of "active imagination"; Symbolism; The phases of the moon and their corresponding character types; H.P. Blavatsky and "multiple personality"; Completing the "partial mind." Chapter Five: Descent into the Unconscious. Hypnosis; The mind's internal barriers; Techniques of "dream study"; Borderland between sleeping and waking; Swedenborg and dreams; Alexis Didier; George Russell and Aeons. Chapter Six: Revelations. Mysticism and reality; Drugs as a means of contacting the unconscious; The evolution of ideas; Retrocognition of the past: Miss Moberly and Miss Jourdain at Versailles; Jane O'Neill in Fotheringhay Church; How does perception work? Chapter Seven: Worlds Beyond. Lucid dreams; Out-of-body experiences; "Odic force"; Psychometry; Kirlian photography; Acupuncture; The Kabbala as a psychological system. Chapter Eight: Ancient Mysteries. Alchemy; Mary Ann South's *Suggestive Inquiry*; Jung and alchemy; The mandala symbol; The philosopher's stone as a search for integration. Chapter Nine: The Great Secret. Israel Regardie and Albert Riedel; The "vital essence" of minerals; Armand Barbault; Thomas Vaughan;Gurdjieff on alchemy; The transcendence of the personal; Matthew Manning and Uri Geller; The secret of the alchemists. Chapter Ten: Powers of Evil? Has evil an objective existence?; Unlucky ships, jinxed cars, aircraft, etc.; Ghosts and poltergeists; Frustrated adolescents and poltergeist phenomena; Connection with ley lines; Powers of the mind:

Thomas Castellan, Franz Walter, Crowley, Rasputin, Gurdjieff; Our hidden powers.

PART THREE. Chapter One: Evolution. Man: the god who has forgotten his own identity; What is wrong with Darwinism; Stan Gooch's theory of evolution; Charlotte Bach's sexual theory; The sleeping areas of the brain; The "robot"; The need for inner freedom; The Outsider as an evolutionary force. Chapter Two: Messages from Space and Time. Ted Owens, the PK man; Space intelligences; UFO sightings; Men in black; Andrija Puharich and Uri Geller; Phyllis Schlemmer and Tommy Wadkins; UFO contacts; Theories concerning UFO sightings; Spiritualism. Chapter Three: The mechanisms of enlightenment. The structure of the ladder of selves; Moving up and down the ladder; Mystical experiences; The right and left hemispheres of the brain; Raynor C. Johnson; The great reservoir of energy; Rodney Collin's *The Theory of Celestial Influence*; Karl Ernst Krafft and Michel Gauquelin; Gustav Fechner; Control of the robot: alertness. Chapter Four: Other Dimensions. The fifth dimension: human freedom?; Charles Fort's investigations; Arthur Young's *Reflexive Universe*; Science and the paranormal; Death and dying; The problem of time; The trick of inducing "inner expansion"; The importance of "focusing"; The concept of the "feedback point"; The need for more consciousness; The "recycling" of evolutionary energy. Appendix: *Electromagnetic induction of psi states*, by Peter Maddock. Bibliography. Index.

COMMENTS:

A sequel to *The Occult* which attempts "to place the world of the 'unseen' in a scientific framework," and to point a way towards "a new stage in the history of the planet earth." Wilson begins with an account of his experiences when he came close to a nervous breakdown; his subsequent self-examination led to the discovery of a higher self which could take control in an internal emergency. But should we be able to call upon these higher selves at will, and if so, how? Wilson's answer, as always, is positive and encouraging. A refreshing antidote to the popular school of thought which sees little or no future for the human race.

The 2006 Watkins reprint ('f' above) contains a new Introduction between pages xxiii-xxvi. The pagination of the book is confusing, however: the preliminaries have roman numerals to xxvi, whereafter the text commences at page 23.

Two chapters 'The Ladder of Selves' and 'The Mechanisms of Enlightenment' were reprinted as part of the e-book *The Ladder of Selves* and *The Search for Power Consciousness* (Berkeley, CA: Maurice Bassett, 2002).

SECONDARY SOURCES AND REVIEWS:

1. Benson-Gyles, Dick. "It's All in the Mind," in *Western Morning News* (Oct. 13, 1978): 7.
2. Bird, C. *Washington Post Book World* 12 (Dec. 24, 1978): E3.
3. Celebration: Chapter 21.
4. *Choice* 16 (May, 1979): 372.
5. Dingwall, J. *British Book News* (Jan. 1, 1979): 20.
6. Dossor: Chapter 6.
7. Hudnall, Clayton. *Best Sellers* 38 (Mar., 1979): 403.
8. *Illustrated London News* 266 (Oct., 1978): 121.
9. *Kirkus Reviews* 46 (Dec. 1, 1978): 1348.
10. Martin, Vernon. *Library Journal* 104 (Feb. 1, 1979): 410.
11. McNeil, Helen. "A Severed Head." *New Statesman* 96 (Dec. 22-29, 1978): 885.
12. Merchant, Norris. *Christian Century* 96 (July 4-11, 1979): 712-713.
13. *National Review* 31 (Nov. 9, 1979): 1448.
14. Pedlar, Kit. *New Scientist* 79 (Sept. 28, 1978): 956-957.
15. *Publishers Weekly* 214 (Nov. 6, 1978): 67.
16. *Publishers Weekly* 217 (Mar. 7, 1980): 88.
17. *Times* (Sept. 28, 1978): 8.
18. Walton, Alan Hull. "Colin Wilson's Magnum Opus."

Books & Bookmen 24 (Mar., 1979): 41-43. (Reprinted in Celebration, p. 130-136.)

19. *Writer's Review* (Feb./Mar., 1979): 4.
20. *Material for Thought* (San Francisco) (Spring 1982): 72-74.
21. Around: 160-173.
22. Stanley: *Literary Encyclopedia* http://www.litencyc.com/

Book 3: *Beyond the Occult*

❀

Beyond the Occult, the third book in Colin Wilson's 'Occult Trilogy', was published late in 1988, both in the UK and the US, by Bantam Press. It was the culmination of twenty years' research into the paranormal which commenced with the publication of a huge volume, *The Occult*, in 1971 and was followed by the equally bulky *Mysteries* in 1978. The decision to write a book about the occult, against the advice of Robert Graves, turned out to be advantageous to Wilson as the books were, mostly, well received and spawned many popular spin-offs [see following checklist]. Indeed, it is difficult to imagine how he could have supported himself and his growing family, post-1970, without undergoing more arduous lecture tours of the United States, if he had not taken this bold step.

Some readers, however, had been alienated by this seemingly new direction in Wilson's work, but a careful examination of many of his previous books reveals, at the very least, a passing interest in the subject. Wilson himself has always considered his 'serious' occult books—i.e. the 'Occult Trilogy'—to be a logical extension of his 'new existentialism', providing evidence that man possesses latent powers which, if tapped and harnessed, could lead to hugely expanded consciousness and potentially even an evolutionary leap. In a lengthy Introduction to the new edition of *Beyond the Occult*, published in 2008, Wilson writes:

"When *The Occult* appeared in 1971, it soon became apparent that many people who had regarded me as a kind of maverick existentialist now believed that I had turned to more trivial topics, and abandoned the rigour of my 'Outsider' books. To me, such a view was incomprehensible. It seemed obvious to me that if the 'paranormal' was a reality—as I was increasingly convinced that it was—then any philosopher who refused to take it into account was merely closing his eyes." (Wilson (1), xxviii)

Beyond the Occult: "unites two main currents in my thinking: the 'existentialist' ideas developed in *The Outsider*, and the ideas that developed from my study of 'the occult'." (Wilson (1), xvii)

He may have left *some* readers behind but during the 1970s and 1980s he gained many, many more. Wilson was, as always, confident and upbeat, describing *Beyond the Occult*, in the first sentence of that same Introduction as "...my most important non-fiction book." (Wilson (1), xvii)

The book is divided into 2 sections: Part One: Hidden Powers; Part Two: Powers of Good and Evil. In the introductory chapter to Part One, Wilson attempts to answer those critics who had accused him of gullibility: "When I began systematic research for my book *The Occult*, I must admit that my attitude was basically sceptical" (27*). As his research progressed, however, he became impressed by the consistency of reports of telepathy, 'second sight' and precognition:

"...in deciding what to believe and what not to believe I applied exactly the same standards that I would apply in science. If something had been observed independently by a number of trustworthy observers, then I was inclined to accept it as fact..." (28)

As a result of all this research: "I arrived at the reasonable conclusion that human beings possess a whole range of 'hidden powers' of which they are usually unaware, and that these include telepathy, 'second-sight', precognition and psychometry" (29-30). But although the unconscious mind seemed to Wilson to provide a "fairly convincing" explanation for some of these phenomena it could not explain some of the "highly convincing" evidence for life after death, reincarnation and precognition. He writes: "There can be no 'scientific' explanation for precognition because it is obviously impossible to know about an event which has not yet happened. Yet my reading revealed that there are hundreds of serious, well-documented cases." (31) He considers that maybe the part of the 'non conscious self' which has paranormal powers is not Freud's unconscious mind "but some kind of *superconscious* mind...as much above 'everyday awareness' as the subconscious...is below it." (36)

In Chapter One: 'Mediums and Mystics', Wilson refers to a recent survey, in which it was revealed that 36 per cent of human beings have had a mystical experience:

> "One thing seems clear: the world glimpsed in these moments of insight is *more* real than the world of everyday reality.... But the main insight of all mystical experiences is obviously a sense of *meaning*...the mystic feels—or rather 'sees'—that the whole universe is a gigantic pattern.... Mystical experiences invariably seem to instil courage and optimism." (42-3)

The mind, however, despite being a marvellously powerful instrument, "is no more capable of *grasping* reality than I can eat gravy with a fork. It was not made for the job." (45) So how can we build a bridge between everyday experience and mystical experience? The answer lies in split-brain psychology, the discovery that we have literally two people living inside our heads:

> "...we...have to understand that we have two instruments for grasping the world around us, not—as we naturally tend to assume—just one. One part of the mind has the power to encounter reality...simply and directly.... The other part can only come to terms with reality by strapping it into a kind of

rigid iron framework and measuring it with rulers and clocks." (45)

Wilson is referring to the right and left hemispheres of the brain: "The left brain is a kind of microscope whose purpose is to examine the world in detail; the right is a kind of telescope whose purpose is to scan wide vistas of meaning." (52)

[Wilson seems to have 'discovered' the results of split-brain research (which was carried out in the 1960s) in the mid-1970s and first made mention of it in the second 'Occult Trilogy' book *Mysteries* (1978). He then went on to apply this to his ideas on human consciousness in a book entitled *Frankenstein's Castle: the right brain: door to wisdom* (Bath: Ashgrove Press) in 1980.]

But it is also important to realise that perception is intentional. In other words:

"...we control the amount of energy we put into perception... Our minds have a 'concentrative faculty', a certain power of intensifying our power of 'focusing'.... This faculty has the power of suddenly increasing our sense of reality; in fact, it might be labelled... 'the reality function'. The 'reality function' is undoubtedly one of the major keys to the problem of mystical experience." (52)

In Chapter 2: 'The Other Self' Wilson traces the 'discovery' of the double brain back into the nineteenth century when Thomson Jay Hudson wrote his *Law of Psychic Phenomena* (1893) in which he suggested that we possess an 'objective' and a 'subjective' mind:

"...the most exciting idea was that the subjective mind has incredible powers—of memory, of invention, of power over the body—and that we *all* possess a subjective mind. Then why are we not all geniuses? Because our objective minds *cramp the powers* of the subjective mind. We *would* be geniuses if we could release these powers." (59)

[In fact the double brain theory is much older than this. In 1836, the phrenologist, biologist and evolutionary theorist Hewett Watson [1804-1881] published a paper in the *Phrenological Journal* entitled 'What is the Use of the Double Brain?' in which he speculated about the differential development of the two human cerebral hemispheres. Eight years later Arthur Ladbroke Wigan [c1785-1847] published his *The Duality of Mind* (London: Longman, Brown, Green & Longmans, 1844). Double brain research was well established in the latter half of the 19th century, as the philosopher of science Anne Harrington makes clear in her *Medicine, Mind, and the Double Brain: A Study in Nineteenth-Century Thought* (Princeton: Princeton University Press, 1987).]

These theories anticipated the experimentation conducted on humans, by the Nobel laureate Roger Sperry, Joseph Bogen, Michael Gazzaniga, and their associates and students, in the early 1960s. Double Brain research became *the* fashionable field in neuroscience, and the number of laboratories focusing in this area of research, proliferated around the world. Wilson's discovery of their work led to him formulating his own 'Laurel and Hardy Theory of Consciousness'. This theory first appeared in print as an essay entitled 'Consciousness and the Divided Brain', published in the journal *Second Look* (volume 1, no. 12) in October 1979. It was reprinted as 'The Laurel and Hardy Theory of Consciousness' in *The Essential Colin Wilson* (London: Harrap, 1985) and eventually as a booklet in 1986 (Mill Valley, CA: Robert Briggs Associates). In it he likens the 'two selves' to: "Laurel and Hardy in the old movies: Ollie, the dominant, bossy type, and Stan, the vague and childlike character." (66) Stan always takes his cues from Ollie. If Ollie is cheerful, Stan is ecstatic; if Ollie is feeling gloomy, Stan becomes depressed (he always over-reacts).

It is Stan, however, who controls our vital energy which he provides in abundance when Ollie is in a positive state of mind. But when Stan becomes depressed, the energy is blocked, Ollie becomes even gloomier, and we find ourselves caught in a downward spiral of negative feedback. "This," writes Wilson, "explains a wide range of psychological states and mechanisms, from clinical depression and neurosis to the peak experience and states of mystical affirmation". (67) This is not, however, the complete story: "There is a third person involved—the entity I have called 'the robot'." (67) Regular Wilson readers will know that 'the robot' is a term he coined for that part of the unconscious mind that performs everyday tasks for us without us having to think too much about it: "The robot halves our work for us. But he also has one great disadvantage. He tends to 'switch on' like a thermostat whenever we feel tired, and literally take over our lives." (68) We sometimes catch it performing tasks that we previously found pleasurable with the result that "experience suddenly loses its freshness" (68) and when Stan and Ollie have got themselves into a state of negative feedback 'the robot' "becomes downright dangerous" (68):

"...life loses its savour; reality becomes unreal. As a result...Ollie feels lower than ever and Stan sends up less energy than ever. In this state a human being lives on a far lower level than he is intended for, and he *cannot escape* the vicious circle for he can see no reason for effort. The result may be nervous breakdown, or paranoia, or even suicide." (68)

But the fact that this can work 'in reverse' when Stan sends up more energy in response to Ollie's positive state of mind:

"...is perhaps the most important single insight that any human being could experience. Peak experiences and mystical experiences are not glimpses of some ineffable, paradoxical truth, but simply a *widening* of our ordinary field of perception." (70)

Wilson believes that this "constitutes a completely new theory of the nature of reality" (70):

"For as long as philosophy has existed, philosophers have been passing negative judgements on human life.... If we can once *grasp*...that our senses are so dull that we are little better than sleepwalkers...then we can also begin to see that when we experience a sense of meaning, it is because our senses have opened a little wider than usual, to admit a wider range of reality.... [Philosophers] insist that we should distrust our senses because their evidence is 'relative'; therefore the statement that the universe (and human existence) is meaningless is just as valid — or as invalid — as the statement that it has an ultimate purpose and direction. But if the insights of the mystics are valid then this 'melancholy relativism'...is quite simply a fallacy." (71-73)

The main problem is with the limitations of everyday consciousness: "...limitations that seem even more puzzling when we realise that they can vanish in a flash and leave us staggered and overwhelmed by a sense of infinite vistas of meaning". (73)

So what can we *do* to wake from this slumber? Wilson is convinced that the key is *attention*:

"...exhaustion and fatigue can be reversed simply by becoming deeply *interested* in something and giving it full attention. It is as if the vital energies, which had become scattered and diluted, are somehow *funnelled* into the object of attention. The moment Ollie murmurs, 'How fascinating!' Stan immediately sends up a trickle of strength and vitality." (75)

Towards the end of the next chapter he introduces us to the important concept of 'upside-downness' and it is appropriate to jump ahead and discuss that here:

> "...when we feel tired or depressed or bored—or simply passive and indifferent—it is because we are allowing our 'trivial' values to dominate our intellectual values. In effect we are holding our values upside-down." (99)

In fact, most of us, by allowing our emotions to rule our intellect, spend most of our lives in a state of 'upside-downness':

> "The chief problem of being 'upside-down' is that trivial values are so short sighted and tend to plunge us into a state in which the difficulties of life seem just not worth the effort...When I am driven by a powerful sense of purpose, my intellect tells me that it *is* worth making tremendous efforts and I summon my vital energies accordingly— or rather, Stan summons them for me. When emotional values are allowed to dominate, my vitality sinks—for it is Ollie who suddenly feels that life is just not worth the effort and whose pessimism infects Stan."(99)

Wilson claims that he has managed to produce these states of concentrated awareness on several occasions and that they: "lasted for a period of several hours, and on each occasion the first necessity was to convince myself (that is to say, my 'other self') that a continuous effort would produce worthwhile results..." (76). This effort convinced Wilson that "...it *is* possible to push our minds up to a higher level of perception and keep them there for a long time." (78). Put simply, we need to learn to raise ourselves "to a level of mental intensity where everything in the world...becomes fascinating." (78)

The remainder of Chapter Three: 'Down the Rabbit Hole'

concentrates on authenticated instances of 'time-slips' and reports, from the likes of Arnold Toynbee, of 'duo-consciousness' (appearing to be in two places at once):

> "...there are times when duo-consciousness becomes so intense that it ceases to be an exercise in imagination and takes on a compelling quality of reality.... It seems to be an unknown or unrecognised faculty, and as such I have suggested calling it Faculty X." (82)

These experiences invariably happen when the subject is in a relaxed, meditative state bringing about a "switch from left-brain consciousness to right-brain consciousness". (85) "Our left-brain perception separates us from reality as if we were enclosed by a wall of sound-proof glass" (88); it was "not made for grasping the living quality of experience; it keeps reducing the world to symbols and measurements." (87) By contrast right-brain consciousness "spreads gently 'sideways', taking in the present moment, looking *at* things instead of through them" (85). Wilson reminds us, however, that we must not consider the left brain as the villain of the piece: "The left brain is, on the contrary, the key to our evolutionary destiny. 'Vision' is important, but control is even more important." (89) We should not therefore try to "escape the limitations of the left brain, but to put them to good use." (91)

Wilson believes that our tendency to 'upside-downness' devalues our everyday consciousness making it "subnormal". He sees 'Faculty X' as everyday consciousness "plus a dimension of meaning" making it "genuinely normal consciousness" (99) and is convinced that it is possible to achieve this at will:

> "We must recognise *precisely* what is wrong with our subnormal everyday consciousness. We must also recognise that our tendency to 'upside-downness' constitutes a major

obstacle to learning to achieve genuinely normal consciousness. 'Upside-downness' blinds us to reality.... The first steps towards achieving normal consciousness is to grasp the mechanisms of 'upside-downness'." (100)

The final four chapters of Part One provide over 100 pages of recorded instances of time-slips, psychometry, clairvoyance, precognitive dreams, synchronicities and out-of-body experiences. Wilson believes that there is such a huge body of evidence to support these phenomena that to dismiss them all as fancy or invention — as many academics, sceptics and scientists do — is, in itself, illogical and unscientific. He is suggesting that there may indeed be more things in heaven and earth than are dreamt of in our philosophies!

He concludes Part One by claiming that he was convinced that "the simple, straightforward answer to all the mysteries of the paranormal was the 'hidden power' inside all of us." (210) However, although he once *saw* this as a "comprehensive theory of the paranormal" (210) he now feels that it is "subject to certain qualifications" (210). These are discussed in the more controversial Part Two of *Beyond the Occult*: 'Powers of Good and Evil'.

In the opening chapter of Part Two: 'The Search for Evidence', Wilson reveals how the dawn of a new decade (the 1980s) caused him to re-think the conclusions reached in his two previous 'Occult Trilogy' titles by presenting the extraordinary poltergeist case of 'The Black Monk of Pontefract', a case he had personally investigated in 1980 and subsequently written an account of in his 1981 book *Poltergeist! a study in destructive haunting* (Sevenoaks, Kent: New English Library). This was the case that changed his mind, convincing him that poltergeists are *not* products of the unconscious mind but, in fact, *spirits*:

"It was an embarrassing admission to have to make...there is probably not a single respectable parapsychologist in the world who will publicly admit the existence of spirits.... Before that trip to Pontefract I had been in basic agreement with them [but that] case left me in no possible doubt that the entity...was a spirit....And I must admit that it still causes me a kind of flash of protest to write such a sentence: the rationalist in me wants to say, 'Oh come off it....' Yet the evidence points clearly in that direction and it would be simple dishonesty not to admit it...the picture that now began to emerge made me aware of how far my preconceptions had caused me to impose an unnatural logic on the whole subject of the paranormal. It was not so much that the conceptions underlying *The Occult* and *Mysteries* were wrong as that they were incomplete...." (238)

[It has not been possible, in an essay of this length, to present the details of this case. Readers who are interested should refer to the above mentioned book and decide for themselves whether Wilson's 'conversion' was justified.]

This implies, of course, that there is life after death and Wilson went on to write *Afterlife: an investigation of the evidence for life after death* in 1985 (London: Harrap Ltd.) in which he concluded that evidence points unmistakably to survival.

In the light of these revelations, Wilson uses the next three chapters to take a 'new' look at witchcraft, magic, possession, multiple personality, astral projection and spiritualism, asking finally:

"...how far does it *matter* whether there is a 'psychic world', whether spirits exist, whether reincarnation is a reality, whether mediums really contact the dead?.... What is interesting about the paranormal is its suggestion that we possess 'hidden powers'. Human beings tend to suffer from the 'passive fallacy', the notion that we are mere products of the material world and that the material world is the ultimate reality. For a large proportion of our lives our consciousness is little more than a mirror that reflects this 'reality'. It is only in moments of concentration and excitement that we grasp that the real purpose of consciousness is to *change* the world. Synchronicities, flashes of clairvoyance or precognition or mystical insight, make us aware that our power to change the world is greater than we imagine. This is the most important insight to arise from the study of the paranormal; this is the essence of the 'occult vision'. By comparison ghosts and spirits seem interesting but not particularly important." (313)

Thus, having knocked himself off-course, Wilson steadies the boat somewhat and steers it back to more familiar waters.

In the penultimate chapter, 'Completing the Picture', Wilson returns to his concept of 'upside-downness', taking it a step further:

"...we accept the present moment *as if it were complete in itself* (327)... If I am bored, that is because life is boring. If I am tired, that is because life is tiring (328-9).... Our underlying, instinctive feeling is that life is grim and difficult and something awful might happen at any moment.... It is not simply that our emotions are negative, but that our intellect *agrees with them.* Our judgement ratifies the 'upside-down' view of the world...." (327)

But, says Wilson, the present moment almost always gives us an *incomplete* picture of life which is in need of 'completing':

"This 'completing' is the most basic activity of all intelligent beings.... But our 'completing' activities tend to vary from moment to moment. When I am tired I may watch television without taking it in: I cannot be bothered to 'complete' it. On the other hand when I set out on holiday the world seems to me an extraordinary place.... My mind is now doing its 'completing' work with enthusiasm and efficiency." (328)

The result of this insight is not a state of constant euphoria but "...a calm recognition that life is *not* difficult..." and that most of our problems can be "...dealt with by using what might be called 'constructive will-force'" (331):

> "Whenever we experience delight we realize that the answer is simply to translate this delight into intellectual terms— words and ideas—*and then trust the intellect*. From then on we must learn to carry out the act of 'completing' with conscious deliberation, with the unshakeable certainty that it is providing the correct solution.... We merely need to grasp this insight about 'completing' and 'upside-downness' to see that most human suffering is self-inflicted." (330-1)

Wilson believes that achieving this turnaround, and freeing-up vital energy, can also help produce the 'occult vision': mystical insights, clairvoyance, out-of-body experiences, telepathy, precognition etc.

In an important final chapter, Wilson delineates his 'Seven Levels of Consciousness'. In Levels 1 to 4, ranging from dream consciousness to everyday consciousness, we are heavily under the influence of 'the robot'. In Level 5, however, 'spring-morning consciousness', we experience moments of bubbling happiness: 'peak experiences'. Level 6, the 'magical level', is when life becomes a continuous 'peak experience'. Wilson calls Level 7 'Faculty X': "There is an almost godlike sensation...[a] sense of *mastery over time*..." (348). It should be emphasised, however, that Wilson is only delineating the seven levels of what he calls '*normal*' consciousness:

"The most interesting thing about the levels beyond Level 7...is that they seem to *contradict* the evidence of our senses and of everyday consciousness. The inner becomes the outer, the outer becomes the inner, man is the whole universe and a mere atom, space and time are seen to be illusions..." (348)

In his autobiography *Dreaming to Some Purpose* (2004) he adds:

"...excluding the weird and paradoxical Level 8, I had worked out the basic normal levels of consciousness. The interesting thing is that up to...Level 4½, consciousness is passive. Beyond 4½, it is as if you have reached a mountain top, and the going is now all downhill; consciousness has become *active*.

To grasp this is obviously of immense importance, for once you know that a certain effort will take you to Level 5 and beyond, you become unstoppable. There is a law of consciousness which states: the stronger it becomes, the stronger it is capable of becoming. And the method involves focused attention." (Wilson (3), 354)

[The inadequacy of language (see below) becomes apparent when considering the levels above 7. But Wilson has always been a great believer in elucidating his central ideas by incorporating them into his fiction and there is no better example than his 1967 novel *The Mind Parasites* (London: Arthur Barker). Gilbert Austin's 'disappearance' after his last great battle with the parasites, possibly to join the enigmatic 'universal police', appears to be an allegorical reference to his elevation above Level 7. The battle against the parasites had apparently "...geared him to a faster rate of evolution...." (Wilson (4), 191)]

So, in order to transform our lives we need to: "...grasp that the apparent 'ordinariness' of the world is a delusion created by the robot..." (359). The key is the 'peak experience':

"...a feeling that life is full of marvellous possibilities. This happens when the subconscious mind is in a positive mood — in which state it is as if we had switched on a kind of rose-coloured underfloor lighting....The peak experience is a perception that all is well and that the 'upside-downness' which usually fills us with mistrust is a misunderstanding, a childish delusion." (359-60)

Wilson is convinced that these glimpses of our "hidden powers" are a sign of our evolutionary potential: "Our chief problem is to interpret these glimpses in terms of reason and logic..." (361). Thus the message delivered in *Beyond the Outsider* (1965), at the conclusion of his 'Outsider Cycle': "The way forward lies through the development of language" (Wilson (2), 183), is repeated here at the conclusion of his 'Occult Trilogy': "The basic weapon in this evolutionary struggle is language" (354). As we learn the method of putting these moments of vision into words "...we become aware that there is a vital link between mystical experience, paranormal experience and the unexplored powers of the imagination." (361)

In conclusion, Mankind has:

"...climbed the world's highest mountains and explored its most inhospitable wildernesses, yet where consciousness is concerned he has hardly ventured beyond his own backyard....he accepts peak experiences as a pleasant kind of bonus instead of recognising their implications: that all life could be a kind of continual peak experience....He accepts stagnation as a norm (for that is what ordinary consciousness amounts to)....

As long as this remains true man will continue to mark time at this present stage of evolution. The moment it ceases to be true, the next stage of human evolution will commence." (362)

Once again, as with most of Wilson's output, reactions to *Beyond the Occult* were mixed. Since the publication of the first book in his 'Occult Trilogy' *The Occult*, in 1971, he had accepted many commissions for ephemeral works and published copious popular volumes on the subject. As a result of this, the serious critics deserted him again and he laid himself open to the criticism of fanatical sceptics like Martin Gardner. When Wilson provided two articles for *The Oxford Companion to the Mind* (Oxford: OUP, 1987) on 'Astrology' and 'Paranormal Phenomena and the Unconscious Mind', Gardner unleashed a scathing attack: "Colin Wilson invades an Oxford Companion" (Gardner, 155-57) in which he lambasted the editors for commissioning articles from, in his opinion, such an unreliable source! [Students are referred to Howard F. Dossor's comments about Gardner's criticism of Wilson on pages 213-215 of his study *Colin Wilson: the man and his mind* and Damon Wilson's Foreword to *The Mammoth Book of the Supernatural*. London: Robinson Publishing, 1991.]

George C. Poulos, in his essay for *Around the Outsider*, provides his objections to the book, singling out the spirit hypothesis to explain poltergeists and The Laurel and Hardy Theory of Consciousness as its weak points and asks:

"Is *Beyond the Occult* Wilson's best book? The detracting elements...would lead me to say definitely not. Nor does it possess the driven inspiration of *The Occult* or *Mysteries*. It has the feeling of a mopping-up operation, a farewell to the subject. You gain the impression that after 20 years 'in the cycle', Wilson has said enough about the occult.... Creatively and philosophically, Wilson had already moved *beyond the occult*, at the time he wrote the book..." (*Around*, 236)

David Tame, in his review for *Critique* (no. 31, June-Sept 1989, p. 86-88) disagrees: "In this reviewer's opinion it is Wilson's most important book to date...". Howard F. Dossor, in his review for

Resurgence (Issue 136, Sept./Oct. 1989, p. 50-51) concurs. It is, however, significant that Dossor concentrates fully on the first half of the book citing Wilson's important theories of 'Faculty X', 'peak experience', 'upside-downness', 'completing' and the 'seven levels of consciousness' as the book's strengths, making no mention of the 'spirit hypothesis':

"Wilson's study of the occult is profoundly important. In an age dominated by an intellectual persuasion that resists even an invitation to explore the totality of the evidence to hand, his work constitutes a major challenge." (Dossor, 213)

Whatever the critical response, there can be little doubt that, when considering Wilson's work as a whole, the three solid books that make up the 'Occult Trilogy' form an important and imposing edifice.

*All page numbers refer to the first edition of *Beyond the Occult* (London: Bantam Press, 1988).

References:

Around the Outsider: essays presented to Colin Wilson on the occasion of his eightieth birthday (edited by Colin Stanley). Winchester: O-Books, 2011.

Dossor, Howard F.: *Colin Wilson: the man and his mind*. Shaftesbury: Element Books, 1989.

Gardner, Martin: *On the Wild Side*. Buffalo, NY: Prometheus Books, 1992.

Wilson, Colin (1): *Beyond the Occult*. London: Watkins Publishing, 2008.

Wilson, Colin (2): *Beyond the Outsider*. London: Arthur Barker Limited, 1965.

Wilson, Colin (3): *Dreaming to Some Purpose*. London: Century, 2004.

Wilson, Colin (4): *The Mind Parasites*. New York: Monkfish Book Publishing Company, 2005. (This edition contains a new Preface by Wilson-scholar Gary Lachman and a new Afterword by Wilson himself.)

Bibliographical details:

Beyond the Occult.

a. London, New York: Bantam Press, 1988, 381 p., cloth.
b. London: Guild Publishing, 1989, 381 p., cloth.
c. London: Corgi Books, 1989, 524 p., paper.
d. New York: Carroll & Graf, 1991, 381 p., paper.
e. [Japanese edition] Tokyo: Atelier Teyotl, 1993, 549 p., cloth. ISBN: 4-89342-189-1.
f. London: Caxton Editions, 2002, 381 p., cloth.
g. London: Watkins Publishing, 2008, [xxxvii, 505 p.], xxxvii, 524 p., paper. [Contains a new 21-page Introduction by Wilson]
h. [Russian edition]. Kharkiv, Ukraine: nk, 2005, 478 p., cloth. [ISBN 966-343-116-4]

ANALYTICAL TABLE OF CONTENTS:

Part 1: Hidden Powers.
Introduction: Why man has lost his 'occult faculties'. How to gain control of our 'hidden powers'. Chapter 1: Mediums and Mystics. Lawrence Lesham studies Eileen Garrett. Mystical experiences. P.D. Ouspensky's experiences. The mind's inability to grasp reality. Anne Bancroft's experience. Split-brain psychology. Mathematical prodigy. Chapter 2: The Other Self. Thomson Jay Hudson. The subjective and objective minds. The Laurel and Hardy theory of consciousness. The 'Robot' and negative feedback. Pessimistic philosophies. The importance of 'attention'. Wilson's own attempts to raise his consciousness. Chapter 3: Down the Rabbit Hole. Arnold Toynbee's 'visions'. 'Faculty X'

and Proust. Sartre and 'nausea'. 'Upside-downness'. Chapter 4: The Informative Universe. 'Time-slips'. The 'tape-recording' theory. Psychometry. Dowsing. Is reality 'out-there'? The hologramatic universe. David Bohm's theory of reality as 'implicate order'. Chapter 5: Intrusions? Hypnagogic states. Rudolf Steiner, Carl Jung and 'occult' phenomena. Synchronicity. Can the human mind 'make things happen'? Chapter 6: Memories of the Future. Precognitive dreams. Time. J.W. Dunne. J.B. Priestley's theories of time. Is the future predetermined? Glimpses of the future. The paradoxes of quantum physics. Time-slips. Do human beings possess freedom? Chapter 7: Minds Without Bodies? Out-of-body experiences.

Part 2: Powers of Good and Evil.
Chapter 1: The Search for Evidence. Multiple personality. Spiritualism. Poltergeists. Chapter 2: The Truth about Magic. Allan Kardec. Spirit healers. Guy Playfair's investigation. Witchcraft—Wilson's assessment of Stan Gooch's theories. Chapter 3: The World of Spirits. Ghosts. Spirit possession. Multiple personality. Chapter 4: Visions. Eileen Garrett. Daskalos. Chapter 5: Completing the Picture. The leakage of energy. Freedom and the 'Peak Experience'. Sex and the 'Peak Experience'. The problem of 'upside-downness'. The concept of 'completing'. Development of the 'completing' faculty. Chapter 6: Towards the Unknown Region. The 'connectedness' of every-thing. The 7 levels of consciousness. Psychic powers are evidence of man's evolutionary potential.

Bibliography. Index.

COMMENTS:

Although this book, designed to bring together all of Wilson's twenty years of research into the paranormal, is largely repet-itive, it does contain some of his most profound work to date. The final two chapters are particularly important. Wilson intro-duces us to the concept of 'upside-downness'—the tendency to allow negative emotional judgments to usurp objective rational judgments. Chapter 1 of Part 2 contains some important ideas on how to overcome defeat and pessimism. As always, examples from his own experiences give his theories credibility and establishes a rapport with his readers.

"What attracted me about 'occultism' was the same healthy element that lies at the heart of religion—that obsession with the mystery of human existence that created saints and mystics rather than 'true believers'."

The 2008 Watkins edition ('g' above) contains a new Introduction by Wilson between pages xvii-xxxvii in which he states: "This is my most important non-fiction book." The pagination, as with the Watkins reprints of *Mysteries* and *The Occult*, is rather eccentric: the preliminaries having roman numerals up to xxxii, whereafter the text commences at page 19!

An extract, 'The Seven Levels of Consciousness', appeared in *Colin Wilson: philosopher of optimism* by Brad Spurgeon. (Manchester: Michael Butterworth, 2006), p. 113-116

SECONDARY SOURCES AND REVIEWS:

1. Dossor: Chapter 6.
2. Dossor, Howard F. "Faculty X" in *Resurgence*, 136 (Sept/Oct 1989), p. 50-51.
3. *Kirkus Reviews*, vol. 57 (Oct 15, 1989), p. 1522.
4. Lint, Charles de. "Researching the Paranormal" in *The Report: Premier Issue*, vol. 2, no.1, (1991), p. 23-25.
5. Shearing, David. "Energy for Life" in *Yorkshire Post*, (Dec. 29, 1988): nk.
6. Tame, David. *Critique*, no. 31 (June-Sept. 1989), p. 86-88. "In this reviewer's opinion it is Wilson's most important book to date..."
7. Around: 217-241.
8. Stanley: *Literary Encyclopedia* http://www.litencyc.com/

Colin Wilson on the occult:
a checklist

❀

This lists printed books only. In addition, Colin Wilson has written many articles on the subject. Students should consult my *The Colin Wilson Bibliography, 1956-2010* (Nottingham: Paupers' Press, 2011) for details of these items.

Books:

The Occult. London: Hodder & Stoughton, 1971, 601 p., cloth.

Strange Powers. London: Latimer New Directions, 1973, 130 p., cloth.

Mysterious Powers. London: Aldus Books/Jupiter Books, 1975, 142 p., cloth. Also published under the title: *They Had Strange Powers.* Garden City, NY: Doubleday & Co., 1975, 142 p., cloth. And as *Mysterious Powers* and *Spirits and Spirit Worlds* by Colin Wilson and Roy Stemman. London: Aldus Books, 1975, 142 p., cloth. (Books bound together but separately paginated.) It was mostly reprinted in: *The Giant Book of the UnXplained* edited by Damon Wilson. Bristol: Parragon, 1998, p. 309-399.

The Unexplained. Lake Oswego, OR: Lost Pleiade Press, 1975, 65 p., paper.

Enigmas and Mysteries. London: Aldus Books, 1976, 144 p., cloth.

The Geller Phenomenon. London: Aldus Books, 1976, 144 p., cloth.

Colin Wilson's Men of Mystery with Christmas Humphreys, Kit Pedler, Oliver Marlow Wilkinson, Pat Silver, Jesse Lasky Jr. and Peter Tompkins. London: W.H. Allen, 1977, 206 p., cloth. Also published as: *Dark Dimensions: A Celebration of the Occult*. New York: Everest House, 1977, 236 p., cloth.

Mysteries: An Investigation into the Occult, the Paranormal, and the Supernatural. London: Hodder and Stoughton, 1978, 667 p., cloth.

Mysteries of the Mind by Colin Wilson and Stuart Holroyd. London: Aldus Books, 1978, 256 p., cloth. [Originally published as *Mysterious Powers*, by Colin Wilson, and *Minds without Boundaries*, by Stuart Holroyd. The two texts are here combined; Wilson provides Chapters 1-7, Holroyd 8-14. *Mysterious Powers* has 8 chapters of which Chapter 7 has been dropped for this edition. Also, there is a short introductory paragraph to each chapter. Several illustrations have been altered or moved around.]

The Directory of Possibilities edited by Colin Wilson and John Grant. Exeter, Devon: Webb and Bower, 1981, 255 p., cloth. [Reprinted as: *Mysteries: a guide to the unknown: past, present and future*. London: Chancellor Press, 1994, 255 p., cloth]

Poltergeist! A Study in Destructive Haunting. Sevenoaks, Kent: New English Library, 1981, 382 p., cloth.

Witches. Limpsfield, Surrey: Dragon's World/Paper Tiger, 1981, 158 p., cloth.

The Psychic Detectives: The Story of Psychometry and Paranormal Crime Detection. London: Pan Books, 1984, 288 p., paper.

Afterlife: An Investigation of the Evidence of Life After Death. London: Harrap, 1985, 269 p., cloth.

The Book of Great Mysteries. edited by Colin Wilson and Dr. Christopher Evans. London: Robinson Publishing, 1986, 493 p., paper. [Reprinted as: *The Giant Book of the Unknown.* London: Magpie Books,1991, 494 p., paper. And as: *World Famous Strange but True.*Bristol: Parragon Books, 1995, 494 p., paper.]

Aleister Crowley: The Nature of the Beast. Wellingborough, Northants.: Aquarian Press, 1987, 174 p., paper.

The Encyclopedia of Unsolved Mysteries by Colin Wilson, with Damon Wilson. London: Harrap, 1987, 318 p., cloth. [reprinted as: *The Mammoth Encyclopedia of Unsolved Mysteries.* London: Constable & Robinson Ltd., 2000, paper. And as: *The Mammoth Encyclopedia of the Unsolved.* New York: Carroll & Graf, 2000, paper.]

Beyond the Occult. London, New York: Bantam Press, 1988, 381 p., cloth.

The Mammoth Book of the Supernatural. Edited with a Foreword by Damon Wilson. London: Robinson Publishing, 1991, 567 p., paper. [reprinted as: *The Giant Book of the Supernatural* edited by Colin Wilson with a Foreword by Damon Wilson. London: Magpie Books (Parragon), 1994, 567 p., paper. And as: *Supernatural: your guide through the unexplained, the unearthly and the unknown.* London: Watkins Publishing, 2011, 567 p., paper.]

Unsolved Mysteries: Past and Present. Chicago: Contemporary Books, 1992, xxii, 426 p., trade paperback. [Reprinted as: *The Mammoth Encyclopedia of Unsolved Mysteries.* And as: *The Mammoth Encyclopedia of the Unsolved.*]

World Famous Strange Tales and Weird Mysteries. Colin Wilson with Damon and Rowan Wilson. London: Magpie Books, 1992, 121 p., paper.

World Famous News Stories: Weird, Funny and Peculiar. Colin Wilson with Damon and Rowan Wilson. London : Magpie Books, 1994, 102 p., paper. [Reprinted as: *World Famous Weird News Stories*. Bristol: The Parragon Book Service Ltd., 1996, 180 p., paper.]

World Famous Strange But True. Colin Wilson with Damon and Rowan Wilson. London: Magpie Books, 1994, 104 p., paper.

World Famous True Ghost Stories. Colin Wilson with Damon and Rowan Wilson. London: Magpie Books, 1994, 121 p., paper.

The Giant Book of Mysteries. Colin Wilson with Damon and Rowan Wilson. Bristol: Parragon Book Service, 1995, 462 p., paper.

World Famous UFOs. Bristol: Parragon, [1996], 167 p., paper.

Strange but True: Strange Vanishings. Bristol: Parragon, 1997, 170 p., paper.

Strange but True: Ghost Sightings. Bristol: Parragon, 1997, 168 p., paper.

The Unexplained: Mysteries of the Universe. London: Dorling Kindersley Ltd., 1997, 37 p., cloth.

The Unexplained: UFOs and Aliens. London: Dorling Kindersley, 1997, 37 p., cloth.

Alien Dawn: an investigation into the contact experience. London: Virgin Publishing Ltd., 1998, 322 p., cloth (published simultaneously in trade paperback).

The Unexplained: Ghosts and the Supernatural. London: Dorling Kindersley, 1998, 37 p., cloth.

The Unexplained: Psychic Powers. London: Dorling Kindersley, 1998, 37 p., cloth.

The Mammoth Encyclopedia of Unsolved Mysteries. Colin Wilson & Damon Wilson. London: Robinson Publishing Ltd., 2000, 662 p., paper. [Reprinted as: *The Mammoth Encyclopedia of the Unsolved.* New York: Carroll & Graf, 2000, 662 p., paper.]

'After the Ball is Over': is there Life after Death? *and* **The Haunted Gardens of Heligan.** St Austell, Cornwall: Abraxas, 2001, 16 p., paper.

Strange: true stories of the mysterious and bizarre. Colin Wilson and Damon Wilson. Long Island City, NY: Hammond World Atlas Corporation, 2009, 192 p., paper.

Introductions, Prefaces, Forewords, Afterwords:

"Introduction," in *The Search for Abraxas,* by Nevill Drury and Steven Skinner. Sudbury, Suffolk: Neville Spearman, 1972, cloth, p. xi-xxi.

"Introduction," in *The Magicians: Occult Stories,* edited by Peter Haining. London: Peter Owen, 1972, cloth, p. 15-26.

"Foreword," in *The Roots of Witchcraft,* by Michael Harrison.

London: Frederick Muller, 1973, cloth, p. 23-34.

"Introduction," in *An Occultist's Travels,* by Willy Reichel. Philadelphia: Running Press, 1975, paper, 6 un-numbered pages.

"Foreword," in *The Power of the Pendulum,* by T.C. Lethbridge. London: Routledge & Kegan Paul, 1976, cloth, p. ix-xx.

"Afterword," in *Glastonbury: Ancient Avalon, New Jerusalem,* edited by Anthony Roberts. London: Rider, 1978, paper, p. 168-175.

"Foreword," in *Ritual Magic: an occult primer,* by David Conway. New York: E.P. Dutton, 1978, cloth, p. 15-27.

"Introduction," in *The Necronomicon,* edited by George Hay. St. Helier, Jersey, Channel Islands: Neville Spearman (Jersey) Ltd., 1978, cloth, p. 13-55.

"Introduction," in *To Anger the Devil: the Reverend Dr Donald Omand, Exorcist Extraordinary,* by Marc Alexander. Sudbury, Suffolk: Neville Spearman, 1978, cloth, p. 11-15.

"Introduction," in *Tarot Revelations,* by Joseph Campbell and Richard Roberts. San Francisco: Alchemy Books, 1979, cloth, p. 29-37.

"Foreword," in *The Rosy Cross Unveiled: The History, Mythology, and Rituals of an Occult Order,* by Christopher McIntosh. Wellingborough, Northants.: Aquarian Press, 1980, paper, p. 9-16.

"Foreword," in *The Essential T.C. Lethbridge,* edited by Tom Graves and Janet Hoult. London: Routledge & Kegan Paul, 1980, cloth, p. vii-xiv.

"Foreword," in *The Dark Gods,* by Anthony Roberts and Jeff Gilbertson. London: Rider/Hutchinson, 1980, cloth, p. 13-24.

"Introduction," in *Clues to the Unknown,* by Robert Cracknell. London: Hamlyn Paperbacks, 1981, paper, p. 5-24.

"Foreword," in *Positive Magic,* by Marion Weinstein. British Columbia: Phoenix, 1981, paper, p. xiii-xix.

"Introduction," in *Healing Energy Prayer & Relaxation,* by Dr. Israel Regardie. Las Vegas: Golden Dawn Publications, 1982, paper, p. 1-8.

"Introduction," in *The Teachers of Fulfillment,* by Israel Regardie. Phoenix, Arizona: Falcon Press, 1983, paper, p. xxiii-xxx.

"Introduction," in *Holistic Healing for Dowsers,* by Leonard Locker. U.K. (?): Privately Printed, 1983, paper, 4 un-numbered pages.

"Introduction," in *The People of the Secret,* by Ernest Scott. London: Octagon Press, 1983, cloth, p. 1-14.

"Introduction," in *Monsters You Never Heard Of,* by Raymond Van Over. New York: Tempo, 1983, paper, p. vii-xii.

"Foreword," in *Witch Amongst Us* by Lois Bourne. London: Robert Hale, 1985, cloth, p. 7-10.

"Introduction," in *Multiple Man: explorations in possession & multiple personality,* by Adam Crabtree. Toronto: Collins, 1985, cloth, 3 un-numbered pages.

"Introduction," in *The Night Side of Nature Or, Ghosts and Ghost-*

Seers, by Catherine Crowe. Wellingborough, Northants: Aquarian Press, 1986, paper, p. v-xii. Volume 1 in the *Colin Wilson Library of the Paranormal.*

"Introduction," in *Death-Bed Visions,* by Sir William Barrett. Wellingborough, Northants.: Aquarian Press, 1986, paper, p. vi-xxix. *Colin Wilson Library of the Paranormal* (not numbered but presumably volume 2).

"Introduction," in *The Haunted Realm,* by Simon Marsden. Exeter: Webb & Bower, 1986, cloth, p. 7-12.

"Introduction," in *The Goblin Universe,* by Ted Holiday. St. Paul: Llewellyn Press, 1986, paper, p. 1-42.

"Introduction," in *The Soul of Things,* by William Denton. Wellingborough, Northants.: Aquarian Press, 1988, paper, p. v-xiv. *Colin Wilson Library of the Paranormal* (not numbered but presumably volume 3).

"Introduction," in *After Death—What?* by Cesare Lombroso. Wellingborough, Northants.: Aquarian Press, 1988, paper, p. v-xiv. Volume 4 in the *Colin Wilson Library of the Paranormal.*

"Foreword," in *The Aleister Crowley Scrapbook,* by Sandy Robertson. London: Foulsham, 1988, cloth, p. 7.

"Foreword," in *Call No Man Master,* by Joyce Collin-Smith. Bath: Gateway Books, 1988, paper, p. 1-8.

"Introduction," in *Arthur: and the Grail* by Hubert Lampo and Pieter Paul Koster. London: Sidgwick & Jackson, 1988, cloth, p. 6-11.

"Introduction," in *Wanderings of a Spiritualist* by Arthur Conan Doyle. Berkeley: Ronin, 1988, paper, 3 un-numbered pages.

"Foreword: Visions and Veils," in *Secret Shrines: in search of the old holy wells of Cornwall* by Paul Broadhurst. Launceston, Cornwall: Privately published, 1988, cloth, xix-xxv.

"Introduction," in *Lord Halifax's Ghost Book* by Charles Lindley, Viscount Halifax. London: Bellew Publishing, 1989, cloth, p. v-xxvi.

"Foreword," in *The World's Greatest Mysteries* by Joyce Robins. London: Hamlyn, 1989, cloth, p. 6-7.

"Foreword," in *Elizabethan Magic* by Robert Turner. Shaftesbury, Dorset: Element Books, 1989, paper, p. ix-xvii.

"Introduction," in *The Light Beyond: explorations into the Near Death experience* by Raymond A. Moody (with Paul Perry). London: Macmillan, 1988, cloth, p. vii-xii.

"Foreword," in *The Case of the Cottingley Fairies* by Joe Cooper. London: Robert Hale, 1990, cloth, p. xiii-xiv.

"Introduction," in *Monstrum!: a Wizard's Tale* by "Doc" Shiels. London: Fortean Tomes, 1990, paper, p. 11-17.

"Foreword," in *Exploring Reincarnation* by Hans Ten Dam. London: Arkana/Penguin, 1990, paper, p. ix-x.

"Introduction," in *Finding Your Guardian Spirit: the secrets of life after death revealed by Japan's foremost psychic* by Aiko Gibo. New York: Kodansha International, 1992, cloth, p. xi-xvi.

"Preface," in *Incredible Tales of the Paranormal: documented accounts of poltergeist, levitations, phantoms, and other phenomena* edited by Alexander Imich. New York: Bramble Books, 1995, paper, p. ix-xxi.

"Introduction," in *The R'lyeh Text* researched, transcribed and annotated by Robert Turner; edited with a Preface by George Hay. London: Skoob Books, 1995, paper, p. 20-76.

"Preface," in *The Archives of the Mind* by Archie E. Roy. Stansted Mount Fitchet, Essex: SNU Publications, 1996, paper, p. xi-xviii.

"Foreword," in *Fogou: a journey into the Underworld* by Jo May. Glastonbury: Gothic Image, 1996, p. v-x.

"Introduction," in *Glimpses of Other Realities, Volume II: High Strangeness* by Linda Moulton Howe. New Orleans: Paper Chase Press, 1998, oversize paper, p. xi-xv.

"Introduction," in *The Mammoth Book of Nostradamus and other Prophets* by Damon Wilson. London: Robinson, 1999, paper, p. vii-xi.

"Introduction," in *The Psychic Reality: developing your natural abilities* by Robert Cracknell. Charlottesville, VA: Hampton Roads Publishing Company Inc., 1999, trade paper, p. xi-xxv.

"Foreword," in *The Siren Call of Hungry Ghosts: a riveting investigation into channeling and spirit guides* by Joe Fisher. New York: Paraview Press, 2001, trade paper, p. 9-13.

"Foreword," in *The Four Gold Keys: dreams, transformation of the soul, and the Western Mystery Tradition* by Robert B. Clarke. Charlottesville, VA: Hampton Roads Publishing Company Inc.,

2002, trade paper, p. xi-xviii.

"Introduction" in *Messages from Space: crop circles bring the first indisputable extra-terrestrial signs from space* by Jay Goldner. Studio City, CA: Michael Wiese Productions, 2002, paper, p. 8-13.

"Foreword," in *The Lost Secret of Death: our divided souls and the afterlife* by Peter Novak. Charlottesville, VA: Hampton Roads Publishing Company Inc., 2003, trade paper, p. xvii-xxii.

"Foreword," in *The Third Level of Reality: a unified theory of the paranormal* by Percy Seymour. New York: Paraview Press, 2003, paper, p. v-vi.

"Introduction," in *High Priests, Quantum Genes* by Michael Hayes. London: Black Spring Press Ltd., 2004, trade paper, p. vii-xiv.

"Foreword," in *Witnesses to the Unsolved* by Edward Olshaker. Owings Mills, MD: Remial Press, 2005, cloth, p. 1-18.

"Foreword" in *The Atlas of Mind, Body and Spirit* by Paul Hougham. London: Gaia Books, 2006, cloth, p. 6-7.

"Foreword" in *I Remember Dying: wonderful true stories of people who return from heaven* by Paul Roland. London: Quantum, 2006, paper, p. 5-7.

"Foreword" in *The Borley Rectory Companion: the complete guide to the 'most haunted house in England'* by Paul Adams, Eddie Brazil and Peter Underwood. Stroud, Gloucs: The History Press, 2009, cloth, p. 6-7.

"Foreword" in *Dark Intrusions: an investigation into the paranormal* *nature of sleep paralysis experiences* by Louis Proud. San Antonio, TX: Anomalist Books, 2009, paper, p. 13-14.

"Introduction" in *Delusion: Aliens, Cults, Propaganda and the Manipulation of the Mind* by Philip Gardiner. Winchester: O Books, 2009, paper, p. 1-4.

"Foreword" in *The Lonely Sense: the autobiography of a psychic detective* by Robert Cracknell. San Antonio, TX: Anomalist Books, 2011, paper, p. vii-xxv.

"Foreword: T. C. Lethbridge" in *T.C. Lethbridge: the Man Who Saw the Future* by Terry Welbourn. Winchester: O-Books, 2011, paper, p. 5-12.

Index

Main entries and subjects are in **bold** type.
All book titles are listed in *italics* followed by the author's
surname in brackets. (W) indicates by Wilson.
Essay titles are listed in 'single inverted commas' followed by
the author's surname in brackets. Again (W) indicates
by Wilson.
Concepts are listed in "double inverted commas."

About the Author

Colin Stanley was born in Topsham, Devon, UK in 1952 and educated at Exmouth School.

Beginning in 1970, he worked for Devon Library Services, studying for two years in London, before moving to Bovey Tracey with his wife, Gail, and thence to Nottingham where he worked for the University of Nottingham until July 2005.

One of the founders and Managing Editor of Paupers' Press, he now works part-time for the Nottingham Trent University and spends the rest at the cinema and theatre, listening to music, writing, editing, reading and watching cricket. One of his current projects involves writing a series of articles about Colin Wilson's non-fiction for an online literary encyclopedia administered by the University of East Anglia.

He is the author of two experimental novels, a slim volume of nonsense verse and several books and booklets about Colin Wilson and his work. He is the editor of *Colin Wilson Studies*, a series of books and extended essays, written by Wilson scholars worldwide and *Around the Outsider*, a volume of essays to celebrate Colin Wilson's 80th birthday in 2011. His collection of Wilson's work now forms *The Colin Wilson Collection* at the University of Nottingham, an archive opened in the summer of 2011.

He now resides with Gail by the River Trent, close to Trent Bridge cricket ground. Their two children, Andrew and Katrina-Jane, have long-since moved on.

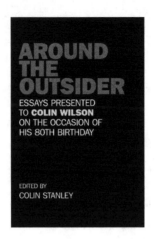

Around the Outsider

A major publishing event by O-Books marked Colin
Wilson's 80th birthday in June 2011 – the tribute
Around the Outsider: Essays Presented to Colin Wilson on
the Occasion of his 80th Birthday was published
on May 27 in the UK and in the USA

Axis Mundi Books provide the most revealing and coherent explorations and investigations of the world of hidden or forbidden knowledge. Take a fascinating journey into the realm of Esoteric Mysteries, Magic, Mysticism, Angels, Cosmology, Alchemy, Gnosticism, Theosophy, Kabbalah, Secret Societies and Religions, Symbolism, Quantum Theory, Apocalyptic Mythology, Holy Grail and Alternative Views of Mainstream Religion.